THIS WAS YOUR LIFE!

THIS WAS YOUR LIFE!

Preparing to Meet God Face to Face

RICK HOWARD
AND JAMIE LASH

Foreword by Jack Hayford

Chosen Books

A Division of Baker Book House Co
Grand Rapids, Michigan 49516

Published by Chosen Books
a division of Baker Book House Company
P.O. Box 6287, Grand Rapids, MI 49516-6287

Fifth printing, August 2001

Printed in the United States of America

Library of Congress Cataloging-in-Publication Data

Howard, Rick.
    This was your life! : preparing to meet God face to face / Rick Howard and Jamie Lash.
       p.   cm.
    Includes bibliographical references.
    ISBN 0-8007-9259-9 (pbk.)
    1. Reward (Theology) 2. Christian life. 3. Judgment Day. I. Lash, Jamie. II. Title.
    BT940.H68   1998
    248.4—dc21   98-17424

For current information about all releases from Baker Book House, visit our web site:
http://www.bakerbooks.com

CONTENTS

Foreword by Jack Hayford   7
Preface   9

1. Encountering the Christ of Revelation   11
2. Take Heed How You Build   23
3. How Do We Bear Much Fruit?   33
4. Lay Up Treasures in Heaven   48
5. The Ultimate Test   55
6. Ultimate Success   59
7. Take Responsibility—But Not Too Much!   65
8. The Fear of Man   72
9. Developing a Servant's Heart   84
10. Stay Out of His Chair!   109
11. The Fear of the Lord Is a Fountain of Life   114
12. Pleasing God in Your Work   121
13. Seizing the Time   126
14. Crowns of God's Pleasure   140
15. Olympic Motivation   148

Contents

Appendix A: Are You Good Enough to Get to
  Heaven?   155
Appendix B: The Vision of William Booth   159
Study Guide: Questions for Group Discussion and
  Personal Reflection   175
Notes   185
Video Information   191

FOREWORD

The skilled approach taken by Rick Howard and Jamie Lash to this awe-inspiring theme is peculiar in this respect: It is both entertaining and frightening. If "entertaining" seems glib, know that it is only in the sense that it is highly readable and engrossing. If "frightening" seems undesirable, know it is only in the sense that one is led to a new awareness of our ultimate accountability for our life.

It may strike some as a superficial generalization to say that every Christian should read this book, but it seems in today's mental and moral environment that it would merit such priority consideration. This book is a sobering summons to our souls—a sensitively discussed but starkly honest presentation that will enrich the reader. We need the weight of such literature to balance the truths of our expectations of God's blessings with the truth of God's expectations of us.

Here is ballast for the soul—a blessing in both smooth and stormy times.

Jack Hayford

PREFACE

In 1987 a friend told me about a video that he said contained the most motivating teaching he had ever heard in his life. It was Rick Howard's video on the Judgment Seat of Christ. I asked if I could borrow it. Since then I have watched that video sixteen times. Never has a single message affected my life so greatly.

I phoned Rick's office to inquire if he had written a book on the subject. Because of that phone call, Rick and I have been collaborating for the last several years to make this book a reality. Our purpose is to bring attention to a truth of incredible power. Nothing in our travels has been so strange as the absence of knowledge and discussion among Christians concerning the Judgment Seat of Christ. Huge portions of the Church seem almost completely ignorant of one of the most wonderful truths in the Word of God.

Understanding the Judgment Seat of Christ has catapulted many great Christians forward in their spiritual growth. George Müller, Amy Carmichael, Charles Finney, Hudson Taylor, General William Booth and Martin Luther are among those who testified to the incredible impact this truth had on their lives.

Because Christ already bore the punishment for our sins, the issue at the judgment of believers is not punishment. God will be looking for things to reward! The rewards are for the deeds done "in the body" (2 Corinthians 5:10). Although we will be in heaven forever, the Scripture makes no mention of our earning rewards after we arrive there. How we serve God in heaven *forever* is being determined by how we live this life! The importance of how we live this life cannot be overstated.

All who put their faith in Christ will be in heaven, but some will receive great reward and some no reward at all. Some will "enter into the joy of [their] master" and some will not (Matthew 25:21, 23). Some will "take hold of the life which is life indeed" (1 Timothy 6:19) and some will not. Some will wear crowns indicating the Father's pleasure resting on them and some will not. This is very serious indeed!

This book challenges Christians to fear God in a healthy way. It is a call to a life of love, purity and fruitfulness—to a life lived with eternity in mind. It is about living in such a way that one day we will hear Christ say, "Well done, good and faithful servant!"

Rick Howard and Jamie Lash

Editor's Note: First-person material in chapter 1 comes from Rick Howard. Both authors contributed content and text to the remaining chapters, but the first-person stories in these chapters are in the voice of Jamie Lash.

ENCOUNTERING THE CHRIST OF REVELATION

1

I was hard at work one Monday morning in downtown Memphis when the phone rang. Mondays were especially busy for a director of Youth for Christ. The phone call was from one of my board members, an enthusiastic layman who always moved me by his consistent witness and love for Jesus Christ. Ed had been an uncompromising friend to me and a great support to my ministry.

"I need to see you for a few minutes this morning," he said in a businesslike tone.

"Impossible, Ed," I replied. "It can't be today. Could we meet midweek?"

"No, Rick, it has to be now. I'll come down and wait for a break in your schedule."

I heard a click. The line was dead.

Ed came and sat in my office as I continued with my work. Then I heard him ask quietly, "Rick, have you ever thought much about the Judgment Seat of Christ?"

I did not even look up from my papers. "Oh, I know there'll be one, Ed. . . ."

There was silence. When I finally glanced up in curiosity, I saw tears streaming down his face. I felt ashamed.

"Oh, Ed, forgive me! Obviously you have something to share that's far more important than this work." Grabbing my Bible, I turned my chair toward my friend. "O.K., what's on your mind? I think I'm ready."

For almost three hours Ed walked me through the Scriptures on the Judgment Seat of Christ. When he finished, he put his hand on my shoulder and prayed a simple, fervent prayer. Then he stood up, hugged me and was gone.

I was stunned. Years earlier Ed had been a Golden Gloves boxing champion. Had he slammed me with his fist, he could not have made a bigger impact on me than he had that morning.

I picked up the phone and dialed my secretary. "Verla, I need to go home. Please line up others to do my assignments during the next few days."

"Are you sick?" she asked in a motherly tone.

"Yes," I replied, "but not in the way you think. I can't talk about it right now."

"All right," she replied. "I'll take care of everything. You go on home."

My car was parked behind the mission. Sobbing and praying at the same time, I drove the ten miles out Poplar Boulevard toward my garage apartment. Twice I had to veer to the curb and wait to regain my composure.

As I drove I was suddenly reminded of a dreadful experience in my freshman year of college. I had achieved a high enough grade point average during my first semester to allow me the privilege of not having absences count against me during the second semester. Without that privilege an automatic grade reduction would begin after three absences in any class.

In my immaturity I had abused the privilege, particularly in one class, which I had skipped for two weeks in a row. On the day I returned to that class, I arrived ten minutes early and was shocked to find all the students already in their seats, notebooks open. My heart skipped a beat. I sat down quickly beside a friend.

"What's going on, Jim?" I asked desperately.

He appeared amused. "You ought to come around more often, Rick. We do a lot of exciting things around here. Today is the midterm exam!"

The shock on my face must have been obvious. "You've got to be kidding!" I exclaimed. Then, feeling foolish and immature, I raced outside and caught the professor on his way into the classroom.

Dr. Rogers peered at me over the top of his glasses.

"Dr. Rogers, sir," I stuttered. "Sir, I understand you're giving a midterm exam this morning. . . ."

"That's correct," he said, frowning, probably knowing what was coming next.

Apologizing for my negligence, I pleaded for one more day to prepare.

Dr. Rogers was a kind man, but he answered firmly, "Mr. Howard, I can't punish you for missing class, but you are nonetheless responsible for everything that goes on here. You must take the exam this morning or receive an automatic *F* on this test."

I can still remember staring at that exam and at my blank answer form with a sinking feeling in my stomach. It was a moment I wish I could forget.

As I drove to my apartment after Ed's visit, that same feeling was in my stomach. A far more serious exam was now before me and I knew nothing about it. I was totally unprepared. How could I have treated so lightly the most important exam I will ever face?

I had been in the ministry for seven years, and a measure of genuine blessing and fruitfulness was evident. But I had never heard even one message on the Judgment Seat of Christ, let alone studied the subject for myself. I entered the apartment and began four days of intense study, poring over every Scripture and teaching I could find on the subject.

Something was about to happen that would boggle my mind—and bring me back to a vivid experience from my youth.

When I was a boy, my father always called me Rick or Ricky. The notable exceptions were times during my teenage years when Dad called me to account for my actions. "Richard," he would say, "give account of yourself!" I knew what he meant: "Where were you? Who were you with? What did you do?"

I would never have lied to my father. I never even considered lying to him (although I did not always think he needed to know all the details!). As I grew older, however, I came to understand his concern and could see the wisdom of "throwing myself on the mercy of the court."

I will never forget one spring evening in 1956. I was in high school and had just begun to drive. My father had recently purchased a new car, a 1955 Chevrolet sports coupe with a black front, white top and back, and white vinyl interior. It was beautiful!—only the second new car of Dad's life. My family did not own our home and never had a bank account. That car was our only valuable possession.

The evening came when I was finally given permission to drive the car on a date. My girlfriend sat up front, and my best friend and his girl sat in the back seat. We were so proud driving through town! I was extremely cautious because the road seemed awfully narrow and the car as wide as a boat. At the end of the evening, I took my girlfriend home first. She lived down a long, private lane. I parked carefully, walked her to the front door and performed the expected amenities.

When I returned, I noticed that my friends had moved to the front seat. What I did not notice was that the front door on the passenger side had been left partially open. As I put the car into reverse and backed down the narrow driveway, a tree caught the edge of the open door, crushing it into the front fender.

That dreadful *crunch* still turns my stomach these many years later. I knew that when I got home, Dad would say, "Richard, give account of yourself." It was a moment I was not looking forward to. Not willfully but carelessly I had abused my privilege. That car was precious to my family, and I was returning it worth less than when it had been entrusted to me.

In just such a way, God's most treasured possession, His only Son, was given at great cost to make salvation and fruitfulness possible. We will give account for what we have done with this precious gift.

Terror in the Presence of the Lord

In the four days I spent studying in my apartment, I read one particular passage at least fourteen times. 1 Corinthians 3:10–15 became dominant in my thinking:

> Let each man take care how he builds upon [the foundation]. For no other foundation can any one lay than that which is laid, which is Jesus Christ. Now if any one builds on the foundation with gold, silver, precious stones, wood, hay, stubble— each man's work will become manifest; for the Day will disclose it, because it will be revealed with fire, and the fire will test what sort of work each one has done. If the work which any man has built on the foundation survives, he will receive a reward. If any man's work is burned up, he will suffer loss, though he himself will be saved, but only as through fire.

On the night of the fourth day, I fell asleep with my clothes on, too exhausted emotionally and physically to change for bed. Several hours later I awakened, my heart pounding and my clothes plastered to my body with perspiration. I had seen a vision of the Judgment Seat of Christ. I had difficulty catching my breath. I was weeping—and my eyes were wide open in terror!

I well knew the scriptural description of the Judgment Seat, but I was completely unprepared for the drama and terror of that moment. The Christ I saw bore no resemblance to the Warner Sallman painting that hung in my childhood bedroom, which portrayed Jesus as "gentle, meek and mild" with chestnut brown locks and blue eyes. I saw Christ as He appears in the first chapter of Revelation:

His head and hair were white like wool, as white as snow, and his eyes were like blazing fire. His feet were like bronze glowing in a furnace, and his voice was like the sound of rushing waters.

Revelation 1:14–15, NIV

His presence was awesome and startling, and He was wearing a judge's robe.

In my vision I saw the redeemed, as numerous as endless waves of wheat in a Kansas grainfield. All Christians of every generation were there. I had been brought up in small Christian groups, so the multitudes of white-robed believers astonished me. As I gazed on the immensity of the gathered Church, I recalled a time when I stood on the deck of the old Cunard liner, the *Queen Mary,* and marveled at the vastness of the Atlantic Ocean.

What came next was not a sight but a sound. I heard two contrasting and clashing sounds. The first was crying—the weeping and wailing I had always associated with the damned. Yet I knew instinctively that no lost people were here. This was the gathered redeemed. In contrast I heard thunderous rejoicing. What release! What praise! It sounded like a thousand Christian camp meetings rolled into one, like the "Hallelujah Chorus" sung by a multitude of choirs.

What an intense contrast!—uncontrollable weeping and unrestrained praise. The sounds clashed like great opposing cymbals: weeping and rejoicing, sorrow and praise—human responses to loss and reward.

Then my eyes were drawn to a group of Christians on my right. I saw a figure among them that I knew to be the Christ. Jesus carried a torch of fire in His hand, similar to an Olympic torch. After speaking to each Christian, Jesus dropped the flaming torch into the pile of stubble and grass at the feet of each believer. What was revealed by the resulting flash of fire brought a cry of sorrow or joy from the believer.

My eyes immediately fell to my own feet, and my deepest fears were realized. Wood, grass and hay were piled there.

I felt sweat on the palms of my hands and cried out, more to myself than to anyone around: "O God, is this all I have to show for seven years of ministry? Have my motives and my work been so impure?"

Immediately I heard these words in my spirit: *Son, look around.*

I quickly noticed that every believer had a similar stack at his or her feet. Some stacks were smaller than mine and others larger, but I saw no one without a stack of grass and stubble.

Just as clearly I heard the Spirit say, *Son, only when all the dross is burned will what remains be revealed. Wait for the fire.*

My Spiritual Mentor

I lifted my eyes from the stack at my feet. I was standing in a small circle of familiar people. My attention was drawn across the circle to the face of a woman who had been very supportive of me in my father's congregation in Sharon, Pennsylvania. Mrs. Shipton and her husband had sat in the front row during every service. For many years she had led the congregation in monthly missionary services, which had influenced my life greatly. Furthermore she had taught me when I was a primary student in Sunday school.

Because I had been born later in my parents' lives, my natural grandparents were deceased and she had always been "Grandma Shipton" to me. She had interceded for me faithfully, and a bond had formed between us.

When I became a rebellious teenager and drifted away from spiritual priorities, she would come up to me, put her small hand on my shoulder and say, "Ricky, son, I'm praying for you. God has a great purpose for your life!"

I would shake her hand politely from my shoulder and say with amusement, "Don't you pray for me, Grandma Shipton!"

17

I couldn't have meant it more. I knew God answered her prayers, and at that moment, that was the last thing I wanted.

One Sunday night during my years of rebellion, I was sitting with some other teenagers in our customary place, the rear pew. We had passed pictures and notes during my father's sermon. But it was usually not the sermon that brought conviction in those days; it was the altar call. Sometimes the sermon lasted only fifteen minutes, while the call to walk forward and commit our lives fully to Christ stretched out for more than an hour.

When I stood during the altar call on this particular night, God began dealing with me. My head was bowed, my eyes were closed and my hands gripped the back of the pew in front of me. Then, instinctively, I knew Grandma Shipton was coming for me! I did not see her coming, I did not hear her footsteps and I had never known her to approach someone personally during an altar call. But I knew she was coming for me.

Soon I felt her hand on my shoulder. Her words were not a request but a command—a command backed by fourteen years of prayer.

"Son," she said, "it's time."

I broke down like a little child as she led me to the altar. I repented and surrendered to the Lordship of Jesus Christ.

During my vision the Lord reminded me of the last time I had seen Grandma Shipton on the earth. She was in her nineties and partially blind. She had become quite senile and often could not remember or recognize my dad when he visited her, although he had been her pastor for almost thirty years. Every morning her daughter, Ione, dressed her, sat her in her favorite rocking chair in the darkened living room, put her shawl across her shoulders and placed her old, worn Bible on her lap.

I had just returned to my parents' home for Christmas vacation. My ministry had taken me to Tennessee and I seldom kept in touch with my old home church in Pennsylvania. During my vacation Dad had said, "Son, I think you should come with me today to visit Grandma Shipton. It's probably the last time you'll see her alive." I accompanied him, although I felt that little purpose could be served by visiting her in that condition.

When we arrived at the simple, two-story frame house, Ione met us at the door. She reminded me that Grandma now seldom recognized even her closest family, but she thanked me nonetheless for coming. While Dad and Ione talked in the entry, I stepped across the threshold into the living room. Suddenly I heard her voice.

"Ricky, son, is that you? Ricky, I pray for you every day. God has a great work for you to do."

I was startled. Was I hearing things? No, Dad and Ione stood behind me, with looks of shock on their faces.

She did not speak another sensible word in the hour that followed. Her conversation was rambling and disconnected. But God had allowed her spirit one clear, unrepeatable moment. She was irrevocably bonded to that little boy through prayer and the vision God had given her for his life.

In my vision a voice, like the sound of many waters, startled me out of my reminiscing.

"Lily Shipton."

Jesus Christ Himself was standing before my spiritual mentor. I do not think I had ever heard her first name—certainly not that I remembered.

"Lily Shipton," Jesus said again. "Well done, thou good and faithful servant."

He touched the torch to the grass and stubble at her feet. It burned instantly in a flash of fire. When the flames had consumed the stubble, I saw a pile of gold, silver and precious jewels at her feet.

She bent over to gather the valuables. Taking them in her arms, she laid them at Jesus' feet and began to praise the Lord. To this day I remember that spirit of praise: "I love You, Jesus! I love You, Jesus!"

I will never forget what happened next.

An Unchangeable Verdict

My attention was drawn to a young man I had gone to school with seven years earlier. I had not seen Todd (not his real name) for several years but knew instinctively why he stood there with me at this vision of Christ's Judgment Seat. We had been bonded together despite our differences.

What a contrast we had made! He was tall and handsome, a leader within the student body at his college. I was a scrawny, underdeveloped teenager. Although he was a college student and I a mere high school sophomore, we had attended classes at the same Bible school and had grown very close because of our mutual spiritual commitment. We each received the call to preach during the same spiritual emphasis week and met frequently for prayer and study from that time forward. Todd often prayed with great fervency for the people of Africa, believing that the Lord was calling him to mission work there.

My friend was dating a beautiful girl from the East Coast. She came from a wealthy family, ranked near the top of her class in college and was selected homecoming queen.

One spring evening in Georgia, while Todd and I sat in his car, he told me that he had proposed to this beautiful girl. My heart sank when he recounted how she had responded: "I love you and I'll marry you, but not if you become a preacher, and certainly not if you become a missionary."

Although this girl professed to be a Christian, I feared their marriage would compromise the call of God on Todd's life. I pleaded with him to reconsider but his mind was made up. Placing his hand on my shoulder like a big brother, he said, "It's all right, Ricky. I know what I'm doing. Don't worry, friend."

Those words still haunt me.

Now, out of the corner of my eye, I saw the majestic Christ approach my friend. The flaming torch He carried was spitting sparks out of its intensity. Christ called Todd by a nickname used only by some of his closest friends, then lowered the torch to the pile at his feet.

Suddenly all was burned. Nothing remained but a blackened circle of earth. That black spot is engraved on my mind. To this day it makes me shudder.

As Todd came to the full realization that he had not pleased his Master but had wasted his life, he covered his face with his hands and began to weep and groan in agony.

I have no words for what I saw and felt. Not a day has passed since my vision that I have not thought about that blackened circle of earth. What a tragedy! Whether a person receives great reward or no reward at all, the verdict at the Judgment Seat is unchangeable.

My Turn

In my vision Jesus then approached me. I saw the Christ of Revelation whose eyes were blazing fire. He stood before me, looked directly into my eyes and spoke one word: "Richard." I saw the torch dropping toward the grass and straw at my feet.

Suddenly I started out of my sleep. The vision ended abruptly. My heart was pounding, my clothes were plastered to my body with perspiration and I was weeping profusely. Moving from my bed to my knees, I prayed during the next two or three hours until the sun rose. I said to the Holy Spirit, *Thank You! Thank You for showing me this!*

That morning I resolved, *There will be a new focus in my life.* I made phone calls. I wrote letters. I got rid of bitterness. I reconciled with people. I changed some habits. Because in the light of the Judgment Seat of Christ, there were things in my life I did not want there, and other things not in my life I did want there.

After the vision I felt washed and cleansed, determined and excited. I began taking full responsibility for my actions, knowing they would count for eternity.

My life has been transformed. It has become more effective, more fruitful, more meaningful, more joyful. Although this vision took place more than thirty years ago, not a day goes by that I do not think about the Judgment Seat of Christ. It really is going to happen!

What does the Bible say about how to prepare for that awesome Day? How do we lay up treasures in heaven? How do we become abundantly fruitful for the sake of Christ's Kingdom? How do we increase our healthy fear of God? How do we purify our motives and develop a servant's heart? In short, how can we live in such a way that our lives will delight the heart of God?

The rest of this book is dedicated to helping you get ready.

(Note: Questions for group discussion and personal reflection can be found on p. 175.)

2

TAKE HEED
HOW YOU BUILD

When my wife and I were purchasing insurance for our first home, I asked the insurance agent, "Do people normally buy enough insurance to cover the full price of a house? In other words, if a house costs sixty thousand dollars, would people normally buy enough insurance to cover sixty thousand dollars' worth of damages?"

The agent responded, "That's what I did."

Since I had not asked what he did, I became a little suspicious and decided to check it out by calling my father for advice.

"It's not necessary to buy that much insurance," my father responded. "As a rule of thumb, people generally buy insurance to cover about eighty percent of the price, because there are two things you don't need to insure. You don't need to insure the land your house is sitting on, and you don't need to insure the foundation, because nothing can happen to them. Even if a tornado destroys your house or a fire burns your house to the ground, your land and foundation will still be there for rebuilding."

This incident brought me fresh insight into the meaning of 1 Corinthians 3:9–15, the passage in which God warns us about the upcoming fire. Let's take a closer look:

> You are God's field, God's building. According to the commission of God given to me, like a skilled master builder I laid a foundation, and another man is building upon it. Let each man take care how he builds upon it. For no other foundation can any one lay than that which is laid, which is Jesus Christ. Now if any one builds on the foundation with gold, silver, precious stones, wood, hay, stubble—each man's work will become manifest; for the Day will disclose it, because it will be revealed with fire, and the fire will test what sort of work each one has done. If the work which any man has built on the foundation survives, he will receive a reward. If any man's work is burned up, he will suffer loss, though he himself will be saved, but only as through fire.

This passage begins by telling us that we are "God's building." If we have trusted in Christ as Savior, He Himself is the foundation of the building. A fire is coming that will test what we build on the foundation, but the foundation itself is not burnable!

The Judgment Seat of Christ is only for judging believers—that is, those who have Christ as their foundation. Since the punishment we deserve was already borne by Christ, the purpose of the Judgment Seat is not to punish sin. Instead, God will be looking for things to reward![1]

Unbelievers, on the other hand—those who reject Christ, the One sent to rescue them—will be judged at the Great White Throne Judgment. They will discover that God is just and cannot overlook their sin.

> Then I saw a great white throne and him who sat upon it; from his presence earth and sky fled away, and no place was found for them. And I saw the dead, great and small, standing before the throne, and books were opened. Also another

24

book was opened, which is the book of life. And the dead were
judged by what was written in the books, by what they had
done. And the sea gave up the dead in it, Death and Hades
gave up the dead in them, and all were judged by what they
had done. Then Death and Hades were thrown into the lake
of fire. This is the second death, the lake of fire; and if any
one's name was not found written in the book of life, he was
thrown into the lake of fire.

Revelation 20:11–15

Will everyone receive the same punishment at the Great
White Throne Judgment? Will Adolf Hitler receive the same
sentence as everyone else?

The Bible says everyone will be called to account for the
deeds they have done:

God will bring every deed into judgment, with every secret
thing. . . .

Ecclesiastes 12:14

Woe to the wicked! It shall be ill with him, for what his
hands have done shall be done to him.

Isaiah 3:11

According to their deeds, so will [God] repay, wrath to his
adversaries, requital to his enemies. . . .

Isaiah 59:18

"I will repay into their bosom their iniquities. . . . I will measure into their bosom payment for their former doings."

Isaiah 65:6–7

Just as there are degrees of reward for the saved, there are
degrees of punishment for the lost. Jesus said it would be
"more tolerable" on the day of judgment for Sodom than for
Capernaum (Matthew 11:23–24; see also Matthew 10:15).
Likewise, Jesus said that scribes who showed concern for wid-

25

ows just to inherit their houses could expect "greater condemnation" (Luke 20:47).

I shudder to think about the fate of those who influence people away from God! Jesus said:

> "Whoever causes one of these little ones who believe in me to sin, it would be better for him to have a great millstone fastened round his neck and to be drowned in the depth of the sea. Woe to the world for temptations to sin! For it is necessary that temptations come, but woe to the man by whom the temptation comes!"
>
> Matthew 18:6–7

> "Woe to you, scribes and Pharisees, hypocrites! because you shut the kingdom of heaven against men; for you neither enter yourselves, nor allow those who would enter to go in."
>
> Matthew 23:13

God loves us so much that He is furious when someone tries to lead us away from Him.

If you want to make sure you will be judged at the Judgment Seat of Christ rather than at the Great White Throne Judgment, please read Appendix A, "Are You Good Enough to Go to Heaven?"

Made Righteous with His Righteousness

If we rely on our own goodness to get us to heaven, we will never get there. No amount of our own righteousness will make us right with God. Our own righteousness, by definition, is self-righteousness. To God "all our righteous deeds are like a filthy garment" (Isaiah 64:6, NASB).

Because God is a billionaire in mercy and kindness, He sent His Son to rescue us. When we put our faith in Christ for salvation rather than in ourselves, God not only forgives us; He also imparts His own righteousness to us! "[God] made Him who knew no sin to be sin on our behalf, that we might

26

become the righteousness of God in Him" (2 Corinthians 5:21, NASB).

On the cross God made Jesus to become sin. That is why God chose a serpent, the biblical symbol of evil, to represent Christ on the cross (see John 3:14–15). When Jesus was made to be sin with our sin, He was cast out of God's presence and cried out, "My God, my God, why have you forsaken me?" (Matthew 27:46, NIV).

All this was done for our sake. Christ was made to be sin with our sin so that we could be made righteous with His righteousness! As Derek Prince wrote in his book *Eternal Judgment:*

> Obviously, where the believer receives salvation on this basis, it would be utterly illogical for God to judge, or even to call in question, His own righteousness, imparted to the believer.[2]

There is no question; the Scriptures are clear. Those who repent and put their trust in Christ rather than in themselves receive forgiveness and the free gift of righteousness. They shall never come under condemnation for sin. John 3:18 says, "He who believes in [God's Son] is not condemned," and Romans 8:1 declares, "There is therefore now no condemnation for those who are in Christ Jesus."

What Will You Invest In?

Imagine your rich uncle is on his deathbed. He wants to give you two million dollars in his will but is unwilling to do so unless you agree to the following conditions:

1. You must spend the money within one week.
2. You must spend it on tangible assets (that is, no stocks, bonds, insurance, etc.).
3. You must keep all your assets at your house.

Under these conditions, would you still accept the money? I thought so. What would you spend it on? Take a moment to think about it. You cannot give the money away. You already agreed to spend it, and you don't have much time. Would you get a new house? New clothes? A new car? If so, what kind? What else would you buy?

Would your decisions be different if you knew a little bit of the future—namely, that there will be a huge fire at your house a month after you receive the money? The flames will engulf everything you buy with your inheritance. How would your spending decisions be affected if you knew about the fire beforehand? Houses, clothes and cars will not fare very well. Can you think of any assets that *can* survive a fire?

How about gold? (The fire may turn a gold bar into a puddle, but it is still gold.) How about silver? Precious stones?

To make wise decisions during our short time on earth, we must constantly remind ourselves, *There's a fire coming! Don't forget about the fire. Don't become enamored of wood, hay and stubble.*

How tragic that many Christians have never heard about the upcoming fire. How sad that many have read the passage from 1 Corinthians 3 but do not take it seriously. God is urging us to invest our lives in things that are eternal.

Last summer my wife and children and I went to a family reunion at the beach. My kids and their cousins started building a castle in the sand. They worked hard and did a nice job. Unfortunately the tide was coming in. Suddenly an unusually large wave swept over the castle and reduced it to a couple of big lumps in the sand. A minute later a second wave hit. The big lumps became little lumps.

The kids did not say a word. I can still picture them, sand on their hands, mouths hanging open in disbelief. All that work for nothing!

Magnify their feelings by a millionfold and you get a sense of what awaits many people at the Judgment Seat of Christ.

Are we building castles in the sand? Empires of wood, hay and stubble? Let's live every day as if we believe God is telling the truth: A fire is coming!

The apostle Paul wrote these sobering words: "We must all appear before the judgment seat of Christ, that each one may receive what is due him for the things done while in the body, whether good or bad" (2 Corinthians 5:10, NIV). Although we will live in heaven forever, the Scripture makes no mention of our earning rewards after we arrive there. The rewards are for the deeds done "in the body." How we will serve God in heaven forever is being determined by how we live this life! The importance of how we live here and now cannot be overstated.

In their book *Living in Light of Eternity,* Stacy and Paula Rinehart write about the effect this truth had on Martin Luther:

> Four centuries ago, Martin Luther said that on his calendar there were but two days: "Today and That Day." He recognized that all the days of his earthly existence were preparation for that momentous day when he would stand before God in eternity and give an account for his life.[3]

The reality of a coming judgment for believers also gripped the heart of Amy Carmichael, missionary to India and founder of Dohnavur Fellowship. In her biography *A Chance to Die: The Life and Legacy of Amy Carmichael,* Elisabeth Elliot describes what happened to Amy when she was just a young girl:

> The decisive moment which determined the direction of her life came on a dull Sunday morning in Belfast as the family was returning from church. They saw what they had never seen before in Presbyterian Belfast—an old woman lugging a heavy bundle. Amy and her brothers turned around, took the bundle, and helped her along by the arms. "This meant facing all the respectable people who were, like ourselves, on their way home. It was a horrid moment. We were only two boys and a girl, and not at all exalted Christians. We hated doing it. Crimson all over (at least we felt crimson, soul and body of us) we plodded on, a wet wind blowing us about, and blowing, too, the rags of that poor old woman, till she seemed like a bundle of feathers and we unhappily mixed up with them."

There was an ornate Victorian fountain in the street, and just as they passed it, "this mighty phrase was suddenly flashed as it were through the grey drizzle: 'Gold, silver, precious stones, wood, hay, stubble—every man's work shall be made manifest; for the day shall declare it, because it shall be declared by fire; and the fire shall try every man's work of what sort it is. If any man's work abide—'"

Amy turned to see who had spoken. There was nothing but the fountain, the muddy street, the people with their politely surprised faces. The children plodded on with the bundle of feathers, but something had happened to the girl which changed forever life's values.[4]

Ready or Not, Here He Comes!

When will our lives be laid bare at the judgment of believers? As the following Scriptures indicate, this judgment will take place when Christ returns.

"The Son of man is to come with his angels in the glory of his Father, and then he will repay every man for what he has done."

Matthew 16:27

Do not pronounce judgment before the time, before the Lord comes, who will bring to light the things now hidden in darkness and will disclose the purposes of the heart. Then every man will receive his commendation from God.

1 Corinthians 4:5

May the Lord make you increase and abound in love to one another and to all men, as we do to you, so that he may establish your hearts unblamable in holiness before our God and Father, at the coming of our Lord Jesus with all his saints.

1 Thessalonians 3:12–13

Many verses about Christ's return make a lot more sense when we realize that the judgment of believers will take place when He comes. J. Hudson Taylor, British missionary to China and founder of China Inland Mission, wrote:

> I saw further that all through the New Testament the coming of the Lord was the strongest motive for consecration and service, and the greatest comfort in trial and affliction. I learned too that the period of His return for His people was not revealed, the important thing being to be so ready for Him as to be able, whenever He might appear, to give an account of one's stewardship with joy, and not with grief.[5]

How Do We Make Ourselves Ready?

A Bible teacher once said, "If you are a believer in Jesus Christ, there is absolutely nothing you must do to be ready for the Second Coming of Christ." This teacher was trying to express the truth that we are saved by grace alone. However, although there is nothing we can do to earn our salvation, God's Word says we will not be ready for the Second Coming of Christ until we have made ourselves ready. The following passage speaks of Christ's bride making herself ready through her righteous deeds:

> "The marriage of the Lamb has come, and his Bride has made herself ready; it was granted her to be clothed with fine linen, bright and pure"—for the fine linen is the righteous deeds of the saints.
>
> Revelation 19:7–8

All Christians will stand before the heavenly Bridegroom clad in the basic tunic that is the righteousness of Christ. Some, however, will have beautiful garments given them because of their righteous deeds—manifestations of the righteousness of Christ within them.

In examining our lives, God will look for the *fruits* of Christ's righteousness, as the following Scripture indicates:

31

> It is my prayer that your love may abound more and more
> . . . so that you may . . . be pure and blameless for the day of
> Christ, filled with the fruits of righteousness which come
> through Jesus Christ, to the glory and praise of God.
>
> Philippians 1:9–11

Nothing we do apart from Christ will be of sufficient purity
to survive the fire. Apart from Christ we can produce only
"dead works" (Hebrews 6:1). But Christ empowers our lives
supernaturally and enables us to do good works. Then He
rewards us for the works that He Himself empowered in the
first place. What a wonderful God we serve!

When the 24 elders cast their crowns at Jesus' feet in Revelation 4:9–10, they are simply giving credit where credit is
due. They are acknowledging that "everything good in me
comes from You. Everything good I've ever done has come
from You."

The casting of their crowns is not a one-time action; they
cast their crowns *whenever* the four living creatures "give
glory and honor and thanks to him who is seated on the throne"
(Revelation 4:9). Continually they affirm, "This reward should
really go to You."

Now let's examine what Jesus says about how to produce
"much fruit" (John 15:5) and thereby glorify the Father.

3 How Do We Bear Much Fruit?

Maybe you have never thought of yourself as "God's field" (1 Corinthians 3:9). James 5:7 portrays God as a farmer: "Be patient, therefore, brethren, until the coming of the Lord. Behold, the farmer waits for the precious fruit of the earth. . . ."

Is it important to a farmer that his field bear fruit? Jesus says, "By this my Father is glorified, that you bear *much* fruit" (John 15:8, italics added). God does not call any of us to a life of insignificance or even to a life of small significance. He wants to do great things in and through us.

Like a farmer, God works His field. If He is at work in your life, rejoice! Nothing He does is of little value. If you bear fruit, He will prune you that you might bear more fruit. He wants to bring you to the place where you can bear much fruit.

One prerequisite to our bearing much fruit, ironically, is admitting that apart from Christ we can bear no fruit at all:

> "As the branch cannot bear fruit by itself, unless it abides in the vine, neither can you, unless you abide in me. I am the vine, you are the branches. He who abides in me, and I in him, he it is that bears much fruit, for apart from me you can do nothing."
>
> John 15:4–5

33

Apart from Christ we can do nothing that really matters. We can earn fame and fortune, perhaps, but we cannot produce the kind of fruit Jesus is talking about—"fruit that will last" (John 15:16, NIV). We cannot make a positive eternal difference in the lives of others. We cannot please God. We cannot do anything God can reward.

Palmers' func.

The First Key to Fruitfulness *atheism p.64*

We will examine two keys to fruitfulness. The first is dependence on Christ. If our works do not flow from the life of Christ, if our works are not "wrought in God" (John 3:21), they are worthless.

OH, MY ACHIN' NOSE!

As a young Christian I had sin in my life I could not conquer. I could sometimes resist temptation for a week or two, but eventually I fell flat on my face. In fact, my face had several rough years.

I thought God was disappointed in me. Over and over I resolved to do better. I became so frustrated by my inability to escape the bondage that I felt like banging my head against the wall.

Victory eventually did come, but it was not by any of the methods I had tried. It was not by my willpower, nor by my determination, nor by making sincere promises to God vowing I would not sin again. Victory came through learning something I had not previously understood. My perspective began to change when I heard a Bible teacher share that Christ is our righteousness. 1 Corinthians 1:30 says, "[God] is the source of your life in Christ Jesus, whom God made . . . our righteousness."

Jesus reveals the secret of sanctification in Acts 26:18. He says we "are sanctified by faith in Me" (NASB). All those years I was trying to be sanctified by faith in myself. No wonder my efforts were devoid of God's power! My repeated failures were inevitable because I kept relying on myself rather than on Christ.

It is possible to believe that you are inadequate, but still continue to look to yourself as the only possible solution. When God called Moses to deliver the two million Hebrews out of slavery, Moses felt inadequate. He said to God, "I don't speak well. Lord, please send someone else" (see Exodus 4:10). God sought to redirect Moses's focus by responding, "I will be with your mouth and teach you what you shall speak" (verse 12). Unfortunately Moses refused to look beyond his inadequacy to the adequacy of God. As a result, "the anger of the LORD was kindled against Moses" (verse 14). Pride lies at the root of our stubborn dependence on self.

I had to learn to look away from myself to Christ. He is my righteousness! So I do not have to struggle and strive to be good anymore. I can rest in Him and rejoice in the truth. The truth set me free! Christ is my righteousness.

Paul speaks about the secret or mystery of the Christian life in Colossians 1:27. He sums it up in just seven words: "Christ in you, the hope of glory."

Have you been struggling with a sin you cannot conquer? Maybe you have been putting your hope in someone who is not capable of conquering that sin. You are not the victor. Jesus is the Victor.

I have had to learn this lesson in different arenas. Before college, for example, I had always been a mediocre student. I was lazy, and my academic record reflects it. I graduated from high school in the third fifth of my class with a 2.7 grade point average. Nevertheless I entered college with high hopes of academic success. In my second semester I flunked every course except skiing. I left college and began a housepainting business, but my business soon started to fail. That was scary. I wondered if I was headed for the gutter.

Then God intervened. He began to teach me once again to focus on Christ's adequacy rather than on my inadequacy. He revealed to me that new creatures have the nature of Jesus Christ, and that one characteristic of Christ's nature is diligence. Christ is my diligence! I began to be transformed by the renewing of my mind.

The results were dramatic. I returned to college with diligence, retook all the courses I had flunked and finished with a 4.0 grade point average. Ultimately I became a college professor. What made the difference? Christ as my diligence.

I no longer try to be adequate. I have the most wonderful peace regarding the future—not because I think I am adequate for whatever might happen, but because I know God is adequate.

Without Christ I can do nothing, but Jesus Christ is my life.

EVER GET DOWN ON YOURSELF?

Do you get down on yourself sometimes? Do you ever get mad or frustrated or discouraged because you are not the person you should be? Do you ever feel like a failure?

I do. I do not witness enough. I am slow to forgive. I do not put first things first. I have missed hundreds of quiet times. (Sometimes I beat myself up over the fact that I have failed God about six million times, but that just seems to make things worse.) I feel that I should be perfect. A perfect husband. A perfect dad. A perfect teacher. Weeds should not grow in my yard. (If you know the name of a good therapist, please let me know!)

O.K., I'll stop being pathetic. The fact is, God has been teaching me something wonderful that frees me from getting down on myself. Psalm 43:5 addresses the problem and then reveals the solution: "Why are you cast down, O my soul, and why are you disquieted within me? Hope in God; for I shall again praise Him, my help and my God."

What a fascinating passage! It contains a precious truth. When we are downcast, we are not hoping in God. We are hoping in ourselves. We think it all depends on us. We are failing or messing up in some way, and we keep looking to ourselves as the solution.

It used to be that when Satan, "the accuser of our brethren" (Revelation 12:10), hurled darts of condemnation at me, I often responded by saying, "I'll try to do better. I'll do better." I *would* do better for a little while, but when I failed again, the accuser was back with more condemnation.

Recently I have been learning a new way to respond. The results are amazing! Now when Satan says, "You're inadequate!" I say, "You're right! But is Jesus inadequate?"

When I answer that way, the conversation always comes to an abrupt halt. Apparently Satan enjoys talking with me all day long about me and my inadequacy, but when I bring up Christ and His adequacy, he no longer wants to chat.

It is not just my words that have changed. There has been a change in my heart. I am learning to put my hope in Christ rather than in myself. I am learning to rejoice in Christ at those times that formerly I got down on myself.

I never have to worry again about being adequate. God does not expect me to be adequate, nor does He require this of me. What He requires is for me to look past myself to Christ, the all-sufficient One, and rejoice in Him. I do not have to strive to be perfect anymore. I can rest. Christ lives in me, and He is everything I will ever need Him to be.

I can be downcast, looking at myself, or I can rejoice, looking at Him. *I cannot look at both!* Looking to ourselves is a form of pride, even when doing so causes us to feel discouraged because of our own inadequacy. We are still depending on ourselves and looking stubbornly inward. But God says, "Humble yourself! This is not about you; this is about My Son."

Paul certainly understood this. In fact, looking to Jesus was his secret. He wrote, "I have been crucified with Christ; it is no longer I who live, but Christ who lives in me; and the life I now live in the flesh *I live by faith in the Son of God...*" (Galatians 2:20, italics added).

Those who are great in God's Kingdom are not great because they have an unusual amount of natural goodness or willpower. The great ones are those who have learned to put their faith in Christ rather than in themselves.

The Second Key to Fruitfulness

God is the farmer and we are His field, but so far we have left out a vital ingredient: the seed. No seed, no fruit. The seed is the Word of God. The heart that bears much fruit (thirty-, sixty- and a hundredfold) is a heart that receives God's Word.

The seed of a redwood tree has awesome potential, but if it does not get into the ground, it will have no effect. The Word of God is an even more powerful seed. One word from God can change your life forever. One word from Him can save you from a thousand pitfalls. His Word is filled with freedom, power and life, but if it never gets into your heart, it will not have any effect.

F. F. Bosworth wrote:

> In the seed there are possibilities beyond the power of the human mind to conceive. . . . All of God's wonderful works are potentially in the seed. By keeping God's garden planted, as the farmer does his fields, a child of God can accomplish things a thousand times greater than men of the highest human talents.[1]

Become Good Soil

In Mark 4 Jesus describes four kinds of soil that typify the conditions of people's hearts.

Some people have hearts of *hard soil* like a worn pathway. The seed cannot get into the ground. Just as birds swoop down to eat seed on the path, so Satan comes immediately to snatch the Word away. It is interesting that Satan would even bother. After all, the chances are slim that seed will take root on a hard path. But Satan comes immediately because he is so afraid of the power of God's Word.

In Jeremiah 4:3 the Lord says, "Break up your fallow ground." Plowing breaks up the soil to eliminate the hard crust, so both seed and moisture can get down into the soil. Brokenness in the believer's life is the humility that says, "Lord, You are God and I am not. You are good all the time. Your plans are better than mine. I trust You." Such respect for God keeps the heart open and receptive to God's words.

Some other hearts, Jesus says, are like *thorny soil.* The thorns represent "the cares of the world, and the delight in riches, and the desire for other things" that "choke the word, and it proves unfruitful" (Mark 4:19).

Still other hearts are like *shallow soil.* The seed falls on a thin layer of dirt on top of a layer of rock. The plants spring up quickly but because they have no root, they are scorched by the sun. They never grow up and bear fruit.

How can we be *good soil* for the Word? What can we do so the Word will enter deeply into our hearts?

God commands us to *meditate* on His Word. One usage of the Hebrew word translated *meditate* is "to chew the cud." This notion may not be appetizing to you, but if you were a cow, you would feel differently.

When a cow wakes up, she soon starts thinking about having some breakfast. Some fresh grass, perhaps? Delicious! About an hour and a half later, she muses about how good breakfast was, and she decides to eat it again. She regurgitates the grass and chews it a second time. *Mmmm.* About an hour later she gets that look in her eyes. *One more time!* She regurgitates the grass and chews it a third time. Only after she eats the food three times is her body able to digest it. If she ate it only once, the grass would just pass on through. But after three times her body is nourished. The food actually becomes part of her.

This is what God wants to happen to His Word. When we *meditate* on the Word, it becomes flesh in us. God may show us something wonderful from His Word, but if we eat it only once, it will do us little or no good.

That is why it is so important for us to keep a journal of what God shows us. Whenever He speaks to us—whether in our own devotions or during a message at church or some-place else—we need to write it down. Only as we meditate on it—ponder it, mull it over, "chew the cud"—does God's Word enter deeply into our hearts and make us strong and fruitful. Psalm 1:1–3 says:

> Blessed is the man who walks not in the counsel of the wicked, nor stands in the way of sinners, nor sits in the seat of scoffers; but his delight is in the law of the LORD, and on his law he meditates day and night. He is like a tree planted by streams of water, that yields its fruit in its season, and its leaf does not wither. In all that he does, he prospers.

Do your times studying the Bible ever become dry? When that happens to me, I pull out my journal. It is like a treasure chest filled with verses God has already opened up to me. I "chew the cud" and it nourishes my soul.

J. I. Packer wrote:

> Meditation is a lost art today, and Christian people suffer grievously from their ignorance of the practice. Meditation is the activity of calling to mind, and thinking over, and dwelling on, and applying to oneself, the various things that one knows about the works and ways and purposes and promises of God. It is an activity of holy thought, consciously performed in the presence of God, under the eye of God, by the help of God, as a means of communion with God. Its purpose is to clear one's mental and spiritual vision of God, and to let His truth make its full and proper impact on one's mind and heart. It is a matter of talking to oneself about God and oneself; it is, indeed, often a matter of arguing with oneself, reasoning one-self out of moods of doubt and unbelief into a clear appre-hension of God's power and grace.[2]

ALLOW GOD'S WORD TO GUIDE YOUR LIFE

As healthy as it is to meditate on God's Word, meditation is not enough. We must also apply it, allowing the Word to guide our lives, as God says in Joshua 1:8:

> "This book of the law shall not depart out of your mouth, but you shall meditate on it day and night, that you may be careful to do according to all that is written in it; for then you shall make your way prosperous, and then you shall have good success."

Think about how an experienced pilot ponders the plane's instruments and guides the plane accordingly. Novice pilots, on the other hand, do not fly by their instruments; they rely on what they can see and feel. In pilot jargon, these novices are said to "fly by the seat of their pants."

A few years ago a stunt pilot took my wife and me for a little ride. He took off, then flipped the plane over and flew back over the runway upside down. In a case like this, if you are flying at night or through deep cloud cover, you can tell whether you are right-side up or upside down by concentrating on whether or not the seat of your pants is touching the seat of the plane. If your seat is touching the seat of the plane, you are right-side up. If not, you are upside down. This focus on feelings—this concentration on what can be determined through the senses—is the mark of a novice pilot.

My friend Mike Waterbury sought to earn his "instruments rating"—a license permitting him to fly at night or in cloud cover. His instructor took him up several times to train him to trust his instruments rather than in what he could see and feel. Mike wore a hood over his face to prevent him from seeing outside the cockpit. His field of vision was limited to the instrument panel.

His instructor said, "Close your eyes. I'll take the plane up and do some maneuvers. When I turn control over to you, open your eyes, look at your instruments and recover to straight and level flight."

The instructor did a number of climbs, turns and dives, then announced, "The plane is yours."

Although Mike could not see out the windows, he felt certain the plane was climbing into the sun. To level it, Mike quickly pushed the stick forward—to the horror of the instructor. The plane had actually been descending. When Mike pushed the stick forward, the plane began to nosedive into the ground at a ninety-degree angle. Frantically the instructor grabbed his own stick and pulled it back with all his might, barely pulling the plane back up before it smashed into the ground.

Not knowing what was going on, Mike scrambled to get the hood off his head. His instructor, white as a sheet, said to him, "Don't ever do that again! You'll kill yourself."

When my friend Jim Blackmon was in Air Force pilot training, he enjoyed aerobatics and flying in close formation at high speed. Learning to fly by his instruments did not sound very glamorous in comparison. But Jim was deeply affected when his instructor played a tape of an actual conversation between an air traffic controller and a novice pilot lost in the clouds above the Colorado Rockies:

> *Controller:* Cessna 123, what is your heading?
> *Pilot:* I don't know. South, I think.
> *Controller:* Cessna 123, what is your altitude?
> *Pilot:* Umm . . . 12,500.
> *Controller:* Cessna 123, minimum safe altitude in that area is 15,000. Pull your nose up about three degrees and start a climb to 15,000.
> *Pilot:* O.K.
> *Controller:* Cessna 123, are you instrument-rated?
> *Pilot:* No.
> *Controller:* Cessna 123, can you see blue sky anywhere?
> *Pilot:* No.
> *Controller:* Cessna 123, O.K., then, nice and easy, keep your wings level and keep it climbing.

Pilot (with stall warning horn blaring in the background): I'm in a stall!

Controller: Cessna 123, lower your nose just a bit.

Pilot: I'm spinning! Help me!

Controller: Cessna 123, look at your instruments and tell me if you're spinning left or right.

Pilot: Help me . . . I'm still spinning!

Controller: Look at your instruments! Are you spinning left or right?

Pilot: I don't know. Help me!

Controller: I'm trying to, but you've got to tell me if you're spinning left or right.

Pilot: Help!

Controller: Cessna 123, look at your instruments! Which direction are you spinning?

Pilot: Help me!

Controller: Cessna 123, tell me which way you are spinning.

Controller: Cessna 123?

Controller: Cessna 123, please reply.

Controller: Cessna 123, please reply.

The wreckage and the body were found the next day.

Many immature Christians crash and burn, spiritually speaking, because they make the same mistake. They rely on their feelings and senses rather than on the Word of God.

Just as the plane's instruments do not scream at us, neither do the words of God. They just sit there quietly and tell us the truth. Whether or not we look at them and act accordingly is up to us.

Hannah Smith wrote:

[Formerly] what the Bible said was altogether a secondary consideration to what I might feel; indeed, as far as I can recollect, I did not consider the Bible at all. "How do I feel?" not "What does God say?" was my daily cry. I was trying to feel before I knew; and instead of basing my feelings upon knowledge, I was seeking to base my knowledge upon my feelings.

I could not possibly feel glad that I had a fortune in the bank, unless I knew that it was really there.

[When] I learned that the facts were far more important than my feelings about these facts, and consequently gave up looking at my feelings, and sought only to discover the facts, I became always happy in my [walk with God].

It was no longer "How do I feel?" but always "What does God say?" And He said such delightful things, that to find them out became my supreme delight.[3]

As we grow in the Lord, we read something God has said, such as "I will never leave you nor forsake you" (see Hebrews 13:5), and we accept it as fact. When young in the Lord, we want evidence to verify that God's Word is true. We may yearn, for example, to *feel* God's presence—to know He is really with us. We are like the apostle Thomas: "I won't be convinced until I feel or see." In contrast, as we mature we come to know God well enough that we say, "God is trustworthy. His Word is all the evidence I need."

Certain truths reside in the hearts of mature Christians—truths that cause their hearts to rejoice. Their hearts are filled with riches: *God is with me! God works all things together for my good! I am a new creature in Christ! Satan is defeated! God has good plans for my future!*

The more these believers call these truths to mind, the more their hearts rejoice.

Satan must get really frustrated with these people. They are hard to deceive or discourage because they keep filling their minds with truth.

After witnessing the Babylonian overthrow of his homeland, the prophet Jeremiah was in anguish. But notice what he did in the following passage:

> Remember my affliction and my bitterness, the wormwood and the gall! My soul continually thinks of it and is bowed down within me. But this I call to mind, and therefore I have hope:

The steadfast love of the LORD never ceases, his mercies never come to an end; they are new every morning; great is thy faithfulness. "The LORD is my portion," says my soul, "therefore I will hope in him." The LORD is good to those who wait for him, to the soul that seeks him.

Lamentations 3:19–25

When we get down, we tend to focus on the bad circumstances and on how lousy we feel. Jeremiah did not get free from his discouragement and depression until he directed his focus onto truth: "But this I call to mind. . . ."

Satan has no power in the truth; his power is in the realm of deception. That is why Satan hates God's Word. Psalm 119:130 says, "The entrance of thy words giveth light" (KJV). In the natural realm, whenever darkness and light clash, light wins. Always. The same is true in the spiritual realm.

The enemy does his work by throwing "flaming darts," lies containing his power. If we believe a lie, it brings bondage into our lives—bondage that will remain as long as we believe the lie. Fortunately God tells us how to stop him:

Put on the whole armor of God, that you may be able to stand against the wiles of the devil. . . . Above all taking the shield of faith, with which you can quench all the flaming darts of the evil one.

Ephesians 6:11, 16

Using the shield of faith means refusing to accept thoughts that contradict the truth. We thus bring God's power onto the scene. God's power is in His armor. When Satan threw flaming darts at God's Son, Jesus put up the shield by quoting God's Word. And when Jesus responded, "It is written. . . ," Satan's darts bounced right off. Lies have no power over someone who knows the truth.

To train my daughter, Jennifer, in spiritual warfare, I began lying to her when she was about six. As my finger moved like

45

a flying dart toward her stomach, I would say, "God has left you, Jennifer! He's not with you anymore."

Jennifer was prepared for her dad's weird game. Blocking the dart with her hand, she would respond, "It is written, 'I will never leave you nor forsake you.'"

I would press on with the attack. "But you don't *feel* His presence, do you?"

She would respond, "What difference does that make? God said, 'I will never leave you nor forsake you.'"

I would try another lie. "Satan has good things for you, Jennifer. Satan wants you to have fun. You've seen how happy those people are in the beer commercials."

She would again block the dart with her hand and declare, "It is written, 'The thief comes only to steal, kill and destroy!'"

Jennifer is not a spiritual prodigy. She had just learned a few Scriptures to prepare for the game. But it is not just a game. I am trying to prepare Jennifer for real-life attacks. Satan wants to destroy my daughter—and you and me as well. I want Jennifer to understand how spiritual warfare works and how she can protect herself with the Word of God.

Millions of people are miserable simply because they are believing lies. God's truth will not only *make* us free; it will *keep* us free—if we use it as a shield.

MAKE OTHERS RICH

Once a given truth is established in our hearts, God can use us to communicate that truth to others. What an honor! With the riches God has put in our hearts, we can make many others rich. God's Word can do for them what it has done for us:

> "Out of the abundance of the heart the mouth speaks. The good man out of his good treasure brings forth good. . . ."
>
> Matthew 12:34–35

Unfortunately many people preach farther down the road of righteousness than they themselves have walked. Perhaps that is one reason so much preaching and teaching is ineffective. A truth has to change our own lives before the words we speak can change the lives of those we share with. Someone once said, "Those who would kindle others must themselves also burn!" Otherwise Proverbs 26:7 will apply to us: "Like a lame man's legs, which hang useless, is a proverb in the mouth of fools."

Jesus said, "A disciple is not above his teacher, but every one when he is fully taught will be like his teacher" (Luke 6:40). Teachers cannot bring others farther than they themselves have gone. They can only work to reproduce the fruit God has produced in them. "Let the word of Christ dwell in you richly, as you teach and admonish one another in all wisdom" (Colossians 3:16). To bear much fruit, we must keep God's garden planted.

And remember, the fruit we are talking about is not ordinary fruit. It is "fruit that will last" (John 15:16, NIV). We can make a difference for God's Kingdom that will last forever.

4 LAY UP TREASURES IN HEAVEN

In Luke 12 Jesus tells the story of a man who invested his life in temporal things and achieved success—in the world's eyes. His labor and investments paid off to the point that it was no longer necessary for him to work. He planned instead for a life of ease and pleasure. What he did not plan on was dying that night.

> "God said to him, 'Fool! This night your soul is required of you; and the things you have prepared, whose will they be?' So is he who lays up treasure for himself, and is not rich toward God."
>
> Luke 12:20–21

When I stand before God face to face, I do not want to hear that particular greeting, do you? Jesus wants us to be "rich toward God." He warns us against selfishness and exhorts us to live with eternity in mind. In Matthew 6:19–20 Jesus says:

> "Do not lay up for yourselves treasures on earth, where moth and rust consume and where thieves break in and steal, but lay up for yourselves treasures in heaven, where neither moth

nor rust consumes and where thieves do not break in and steal."

It must sadden and amaze the Lord to watch so many people running after earthly things, pursuing sticks and stubble rather than the eternal treasures of God.

If a Christian builds entirely with wood, hay and stubble, then nothing will survive the fire. First Corinthians 3:15 describes this scenario: "If any man's work is burned up, he will suffer loss, though he himself will be saved, but only as through fire." Such a person will be like a man who barely escapes from his burning house. His clothes are singed and the smell of smoke is on his body. He is grateful to be alive. But then he turns around and watches everything he has worked for turn into ashes.

He is saved on the same basis any of us are saved—by faith in Jesus Christ. Salvation is a free gift. But this person will spend eternity with no reward.

When I stand at the Judgment Seat of Christ,
And He shows His plan for me,
The plan of my life as it might have been,
Had He had His way—and I see
How I blocked Him here, and checked Him there,
And I would not yield my will,
Will there be grief in my Savior's eyes,
Grief though He loves me still?
Would He have me rich and I stand there poor,
Stripped of all but His grace,
While memory runs like a hunted thing
Down the paths I cannot retrace?
Lord, of the years that are left to me,
I give them to Thy hand;
Take me and break me and mold me
To the pattern that Thou hast planned!

Author unknown

Perhaps the young man in Rick's vision who stood before the blackened circle of earth had earned some reward during his youth, but lost it when he drifted away from God's purposes for his life. Although the ruling at the Judgment Seat is final and the rewards received there are eternal, the Scripture speaks of the possibility of our losing rewards while we are still in the body. John writes, "Look to yourselves, that you may not lose what you have worked for, but may win a full reward" (2 John 8). And Jesus says, "I am coming soon; hold fast what you have, so that no one may seize your crown" (Revelation 3:11).

Which Treasure Will You Seek?

Esau is a scriptural example of one who had an acute case of shortsightedness:

> Once when Jacob was boiling pottage, Esau came in from the field, and he was famished. And Esau said to Jacob, "Let me eat some of that red pottage, for I am famished!" . . . Jacob said, "First sell me your birthright." Esau said, "I am about to die; of what use is a birthright to me?" Jacob said, "Swear to me first." So he swore to him, and sold his birthright to Jacob. Then Jacob gave Esau bread and pottage of lentils, and he ate and drank, and rose and went his way. Thus Esau despised his birthright.
>
> Genesis 25:29–34

The writer of Hebrews warns us not to make the same mistake:

> See to it that no one . . . be immoral or irreligious like Esau, who sold his birthright for a single meal. For you know that afterward, when he desired to inherit the blessing, he was rejected, for he found no chance to repent, though he sought it with tears.
>
> Hebrews 12:15–17

Esau "despised his birthright" in the sense that he regarded it lightly. Later, when he realized the magnitude and permanence of his decision, he regretted it with tears.

Would God have forgiven Esau for selling his birthright? Of course. If people confess their sin, God is always willing to forgive. But God's forgiveness of Esau would not change the fact that Esau had sold his birthright. It would not get his birthright back for him.

Have we been more foolish than Esau? Have we despised something much more valuable than a birthright? If, like Esau, we place a high value on temporal things and regard eternal things lightly, then we will weep at the Judgment Seat because of the permanent consequences of our decisions.[1] The past can be forgiven, but it cannot be changed.

Moses, on the other hand, is a good example of one who did not allow himself to be enamored of temporal things. Raised as the son of Pharaoh's daughter, Moses could have had everything the world has to offer, including wealth, pleasure, status and fame. But apparently he recognized all these as wood, hay and stubble. Hebrews 11:26 says that Moses "considered abuse suffered for the Christ greater wealth than the treasures of Egypt, for he looked to the reward." His heart was to please his God. He wanted the treasure that lasts forever.

Is It Selfish to Seek Reward?

Before learning about the Judgment Seat of Christ, I remember telling God, "I don't want a reward. I just want to serve You." I thought at the time that it sounded very noble, but now I realize I was ignorant, and perhaps a bit disrespectful. It was like saying to God, "These hundred Scriptures about reward are a waste of paper. They are of no value to me."

A woman saw me working on this book and asked what it was about. When she learned that the topic was the Judgment

Seat and eternal reward, she said, "I'm not concerned about reward. I'll be satisfied just being in heaven."

I thought of a good answer for her—about three years later.

"Not concerned about reward? Do you think that just because you get into heaven, everything's going to be fine? Don't you realize the Bible says Jesus will be ashamed of some of us [Mark 8:38]? Don't you realize some of us will shrink back from Him in shame or terror because we're not prepared [1 John 2:28]? You treat God's rewards as if they don't matter, but the Bible says they are worth enduring suffering, false accusation, exclusion and hatred for [Luke 6:22–23]. Indeed, they are worth dying for [Revelation 2:10]!"

Some people think it is selfish to seek any reward. It is not selfish. Jesus commands it (see Matthew 6:1–20)! It is a healthy ambition, a holy calling, one that frees us from selfishness. It trains us to seek the pleasure and glory of God.

Those rich in heavenly reward will not be sifting gold coins through their fingers as they giggle uncontrollably. They will be rich in God's pleasure, able to enter into the joy of their Master. They will enjoy wonderful intimacy with God. They will be useful to Him. They will be able to "take hold of the life which is life indeed" (1 Timothy 6:19).

Even now, in this life, Christians who seek first God's Kingdom experience a foretaste of their reward: joy, usefulness, purposefulness, the delight of God's presence and a sense of His pleasure. These things are not enjoyed by Christians who live only for themselves.

Knowledge of the Judgment Seat motivates us to live wholly unto the Lord and to lay down our lives for others, without expecting something from them in return. God tells us about the Judgment Seat to inspire us to seek His pleasure without worrying about the way others treat us or what they may think of us. Jesus says:

> "If you love those who love you, what credit is that to you? For even sinners love those who love them. . . . But love your

enemies, and do good, and lend, expecting nothing in return; and your reward will be great, and you will be sons of the Most High; for he is kind to the ungrateful and the selfish."

Luke 6:32, 35

The more we understand the Judgment Seat, the more zeal we will have to do things for people who cannot pay us back. Jesus gives these instructions:

"When you give a dinner or a banquet, do not invite your friends or your brothers or your kinsmen or rich neighbors, lest they also invite you in return, and you be repaid. But when you give a feast, invite the poor, the maimed, the lame, the blind, and you will be blessed, because they cannot repay you. You will be repaid at the resurrection of the just."

Luke 14:12–14

Jesus is raising up people who are "zealous for good deeds" (Titus 2:14). In Mark Littleton's words, these are people "who burst with a passion for helping others."[2] Those who will be rich in heaven are those "rich in good deeds" on the earth, as Paul writes:

Command those who are rich in this present world not to be arrogant nor to put their hope in wealth, which is so uncertain, but to put their hope in God, who richly provides us with everything for our enjoyment. Command them to do good, to be rich in good deeds, and to be generous and willing to share. In this way they will lay up treasure for themselves as a firm foundation for the coming age, so that they may take hold of the life that is truly life.

1 Timothy 6:17–19, NIV

As new creatures in Christ, we have been designed "for good works, which God prepared beforehand, that we should walk in them" (Ephesians 2:10). The danger is that temporal concerns will crowd out the eternal from our consciousness.

Take a moment to consider how you spent the last 24 hours. How much was invested in the temporal? How much in the eternal?

Reflecting God's Glory

After a seminar on the Judgment Seat, a woman asked, "But won't all Christians be perfect in heaven?" She thought everyone's experience of heaven should be equal because we will all be equally perfect there.

The Bible teaches that our experience of heaven will depend on how we live our lives on earth. While all Christians *will* be perfect in heaven, not all will reflect the same amount of God's power and glory. Lightbulbs may be perfect, but not all shine with the same power. Some are one-quarter-watt nightlights; some are thirty watts, some are sixty and some are one hundred.

Daniel 12:3, an incredible passage, speaks to this very issue: "And those who are wise shall shine like the brightness of the firmament; and those who turn many to righteousness, like the stars for ever and ever."

How much joy would have to be inside a person for that person to shine like a star forever? How much of God's glory would have to be inside? Would you like to find out?

Lord God, make us wise with Your wisdom. Forgive us our foolish tendency to forget what is important. Have mercy on us, Lord. Don't let us die and then regret the way we lived. Change us, Lord. Make us delightful in Your eyes. May the Lord Jesus live His life out fully through us. May people see Your kindness in our eyes, in our words and in our actions. Work through us to advance Your Kingdom in mighty ways! Amen.

5 THE ULTIMATE TEST

When you were a student, did you ever go to an exam feeling confident, knowing you were prepared? On the other hand, can you remember a time that you were unprepared and knew you were in big trouble?

Exams are not something teachers concoct as a way to make their students miserable, but rather to spur them on to achieve their potential. My students seem to learn more in the three days prior to a test than they do in the three weeks before! When a test is announced, amazing things happen. The glazed looks disappear from their eyes. Those who are sleeping wake up. The comatose regain consciousness. Knowing an exam is coming has a way of inspiring people to prepare.

Like all teachers who really care about their students, God would receive no pleasure from our doing poorly on His test. He instructs us about the Judgment Seat in advance because He yearns for us to do well there. God wants us to approach the Judgment Seat with confidence. First John 2:28 speaks of this: "And now, little children, abide in him, so that when he appears we may have confidence and not shrink from him in shame at his coming."

It is encouraging to realize that every act of kindness, even giving a drink of cold water, will be rewarded (see Matthew 10:42). God will reward us for treating others the way we would like to be treated—welcoming the stranger, feeding the hungry, ministering to the sick, befriending those in prison, visiting "orphans and widows in their affliction" (James 1:27). The activities God will reward are things each of us can do.

On occasion, when I taught a college Sunday school class, my talk was not nearly as effective as it could have been because I was not well-prepared. Sometimes I was angry at myself as I drove home. One day as I was wallowing in self-criticism and discouragement, the Lord pointed out to me that if I kept dwelling on the past, I would miss the upcoming opportunity to love my wife and children when I got home. As soon as I changed my focus, the discouragement disappeared.

Although we have fallen short many times, let's forget what lies behind and press on! There will be a fresh opportunity to please God in the next few minutes. How are we going to treat the custodian at work? The clerk at the grocery store? The new neighbors across the street?

Unveiling the Full Repercussions

In the classic movie "It's a Wonderful Life," an angel is sent to keep a despondent George Bailey from committing suicide. The angel accomplishes his mission by showing George how his life has affected many others for good. He reveals what the town would have been like if George had never been born. The angel muses, "Strange, isn't it? Each man's life touches so many other lives. When he isn't around, he leaves an awful hole, doesn't he?"

How much more astounding it will be when Jesus reviews our lives with us at the Judgment Seat, unveiling the full repercussions of each act of kindness, of each word of encouragement, of each dollar given to His Kingdom's work. We may discover, for example, that helping one friend to find salvation has, through the generations, resulted in the salvation of a thousand others. If only we could realize how much this life matters!

The Lord says, "I the LORD search the mind and try the heart, to give to every man according to his ways, according to the fruit of his doings" (Jeremiah 17:10). God examines and rewards not only our "doings" but also the "fruit of our doings."

Imagine being surrounded by thousands of dominoes standing on end. Whenever you show God's kindness to someone, you knock over a single domino. Sometimes only one domino falls and that is the end of the story. But sometimes that domino hits another, which hits another, and so on. You cannot predict what will happen. Perhaps God will touch another person's heart deeply and your act of kindness will cause hundreds to be blessed.

That is what happened to Walter Maier, one of the great Bible teachers in the early part of this century. Maier's radio broadcast, "Bringing Christ to the Nations," greatly helped John Haggai, founder of the Haggai Institute for Advanced Leadership Training in Singapore, when he was a teenager. One day John sent a letter and two dollars to help Dr. Maier's ministry. A few days later the young man received a personal, two-page typewritten letter in return, answering his letter in detail. John was so astounded that he resolved in his heart, *When I get older, if anyone writes me, I shall be as kind to them as Dr. Maier has been to me.*[1]

When we sow good seed, we may or may not see the harvest during this life. But the fact remains that "in due season we shall reap, if we do not lose heart" (Galatians 6:9). Likewise, according to 2 Corinthians 9:6: "He who sows sparingly will also reap sparingly, and he who sows bountifully will also reap bountifully."

The Sin of Doing Nothing

What if a person sows nothing? Several of Jesus' parables describe servants left in charge of their master's resources. Let's examine Matthew 25:14–21 (NIV):

> "[The Lord's coming] will be like a man going on a journey, who called his servants and entrusted his property to them. To one he gave five talents of money, to another two talents, and to another one talent, each according to his ability. Then he went on his journey. The man who had received the five talents went at once and put his money to work and gained five more. So also, the one with the two talents gained two more. But the man who had received the one talent went off, dug a hole in the ground and hid his master's money.
>
> "After a long time the master of those servants returned and settled accounts with them. The man who had received the five talents brought the other five. 'Master,' he said, 'you entrusted me with five talents. See, I have gained five more.'
>
> "His master replied, 'Well done, good and faithful servant! You have been faithful with a few things; I will put you in charge of many things. Come and share your master's happiness!'"

The second servant, who had earned two additional talents, received the same reply. But the third servant, who had buried his talent instead of using it for his master, is called a "wicked, lazy servant" (verse 26). He is *not* invited to share his master's happiness, and his opportunity for using his talent is removed.

Interestingly, this third servant did nothing immoral. He just did not do anything at all.

If our lives are presently devoid of good deeds, the solution is not to get busy. The solution is deeper because the problem is deeper. It involves a change in our hearts. Evil deeds and a lack of good deeds spring from harboring the wrong purpose.

In the next chapter we discuss the purposes of the heart.

6 ULTIMATE SUCCESS

Imagine that I am a basketball player on the bench in the championship game. When we are down by two points and have three minutes left to play, my coach uses his last time-out to put me back into the game. Unfortunately he does not know that I, being a very tall person, accidentally smashed my head on a ceiling pipe in the locker room during half-time and have become confused. I now think the object of the game is not to shoot baskets but to touch as many of the painted lines as possible with my feet.

The whistle is blown. I become a flurry of activity, and the crowd responds with a roar. As I touch more and more lines, the roar becomes deafening.

When the game ends, I walk off the court exhausted. Reporters and TV cameramen shun the other players and surround me, shoving microphones into my face. I think, *I knew I did well, but I didn't know I did this well!* Then a reporter asks me the first question: "What in the world were you doing out there?"

My coach and I have a little meeting the next day. After he shows me the game films, I exclaim, "Coach, I touched more lines than anyone else out there!" My coach, however, does not seem excited about my accomplishment. He just mutters something about scoring points and puts his head into his hands.

I admit this is a silly story, but the fact is, God put us on this earth for a purpose. We are breathing at this very moment because there is a reason for us to be alive—namely, to please and glorify Him. If our intention is to do something else instead—to amass wealth, for example, or to impress others—our activities will be as absurd as touching the painted lines with our feet. We may be very good at it; we may even set a new world record for touching painted lines. But unless we correct our goal, we will waste our entire lives. We can become so busy that we do not even consider the reason for our existence. The Bible says, "There is one God, the Father, from whom are all things and *for whom we exist*" (1 Corinthians 8:6, italics added). And, "Thou hast created all things, and *for thy pleasure* they are and were created" (Revelation 4:11, KJV, italics added).

If we adopt another purpose, a false purpose, we may not sense something is wrong since we have a reason to get up in the morning. We feel motivated as we busily pursue our goal. But what good is it for us to be successful in any other endeavor if we fail to please the One for whom we exist?

If We Gratify or Fortify, We Die

Like many people, I sometimes fear that I will be short-changed if I live to please God rather than myself. At those times I do not trust in God's goodness.

If a sheep has a shepherd who is kind and wise and strong, then the sheep does not have to look out for himself. His heart can trust. He does not strike out on his own, searching for new pasture, thinking his shepherd might be withholding something good from him. Nor does he need to strategize to protect himself from predator attacks. He just needs to stay close to the shepherd, listen to the shepherd, obey the shepherd.

It is no chore to do so! He loves the shepherd. If you could hear the sheep's thoughts, you would hear something like this: *He makes me lie down in green pastures; he leads me by still waters; he restores my soul; my cup overflows!*

Isaiah declares, "[God] is like a shepherd feeding his flock, gathering lambs in his arms, holding them against his breast" (Isaiah 40:11, JB).

When I stop trusting God and seek to please myself, my endeavor backfires. Instead of finding happiness, I find misery instead. When I live to please God, on the other hand, giving myself away in service to others, I experience deep fulfillment. In both cases my experience bears out the truth of Jesus' words: "He who finds his life will lose it, and he who loses his life for my sake will find it" (Matthew 10:39).

If my primary concern is to gratify myself, then pleasure is my god. I am vulnerable, like a child who will do anything to get candy—even hopping into the car of a stranger despite his parents' warnings.

Living for ourselves can take the form of either self-gratification or self-preservation. Jesus also warns us, therefore, not to adopt the goal of preserving our own lives: "For whoever would save his life will lose it, and whoever loses his life for my sake will find it" (Matthew 16:25).

Imagine being in the shoes of Shadrach, Meshach or Abednego! King Nebuchadnezzar made a huge idol of gold, and then announced, "Whoever does not fall down and worship shall immediately be cast into a burning fiery furnace" (Daniel 3:6). Not surprisingly, everybody fell down and worshiped. Everybody but Shadrach, Meshach and Abednego. Their courage and God's miraculous deliverance have inspired God's people for generations. And it all took place because they did not seek to protect their own lives, but to please and honor their God.

Likewise, Paul determined not to live to save his own skin. He anticipated standing before the Lord and wanted to do so without shame. He wrote:

> It is my eager expectation and hope that I shall not be at all ashamed, but that with full courage now as always Christ will be honored in my body, whether by life or by death.
>
> Philippians 1:20

Our lives do not have to be in physical danger for us to adopt this wrong goal. When I am criticized, I often seek to defend myself rather than to please God. My heart becomes hardened and I shield myself verbally. When I am wise enough to correct my goal, it no longer seems important to protect my fragile ego. It seems important only to please God and become the person He wants me to be.

Self-preservation can take a number of different forms. Protecting ourselves from pain can become our top priority, especially if we have been deeply hurt in the past. A teenage girl once told me, "I haven't been close to anybody since I was nine. That's when my father abandoned my family. I decided then that I would *never* be hurt that way again. If anyone tries to get too close, I withdraw." She lives in emotional isolation—a prison of her own making.

Life, on the other hand, comes only from giving ourselves away in love to God and others. If our primary goal is to please or protect ourselves, we cut ourselves off from life.

When my kids were small, I sometimes got into a survival mode when I took care of them for an extended period of time ("I must survive until Marcy returns!"). I lost all creativity and initiative, and simply reacted to situations as they arose. My mind was not on the interests of my kids, but on myself. Everything annoyed me. Life was miserable. But when I stopped trying just to survive and decided to please God by laying down my life for my kids, everything changed. I stopped thinking, *I'd be O.K. if I could just have five minutes without their asking for something,* and began thinking, *What would I like to do if I were a two-year-old? A five-year-old? An eight-year-old?*

As I sought to bless my kids, I experienced God's joy. In fact, I am frequently amazed at the transformation that takes place when I simply change my purpose.

Our Secret Intentions

The intention or purpose of our hearts determines the direction of our whole lives, much as a rudder determines the direction of a ship. For this reason the intention of our hearts is central to God's evaluation of our lives at the Judgment Seat: "The Lord . . . will bring to light the things now hidden in darkness and will disclose the purposes of the heart. Then every man will receive his commendation from God" (1 Corinthians 4:5).

Everything we do has a purpose. The purpose we adopt gives birth to our behavior. If pleasing God is our driving force, will we lie, steal or seek revenge? Obviously not. Sin grabs hold of us when we allow another purpose to displace the purpose of pleasing God. Maintaining the purpose of pleasing God thus protects us from going off course.

A ship captain stays on course by adjusting the rudder as needed. Likewise, as Christians we can stay on course only by adjusting our rudder—the intention of our hearts.

We first assess our intention by asking, *What is driving me to do what I'm doing? What end am I really seeking?* We may discover we are off course by identifying thoughts that revolve around an ungodly purpose—thoughts such as *What would make me look good in this situation?* If so, we are in danger of wasting our lives—unless we correct our courses. The ship may be running well and making wonderful time, but if it is headed in the wrong direction, what good is that?

When our intention is not to please God, we are not only wasting time; we are rebelling against God, whether we are conscious of it or not. We need to repent. Many people repent of wrong behavior but not of the wrong purpose that gave birth to it. Not surprisingly, they soon repeat the behavior.

Even if there is nothing objectionable in our behavior, that is no guarantee that our hearts are right with God. Behavior is not the issue. The real issue is whether the intention of our hearts is to please Him. To correct our course, we must purpose in our hearts to please God.

J. C. Ryle talks about those who are zealous to please God:

> A zealous man . . . is pre-eminently a man of one thing. It is not enough to say that he is earnest, hearty, uncompromising, thorough-going, whole-hearted, fervent in spirit. He only sees one thing, he cares for one thing, he lives for one thing, he is swallowed up in one thing; and that one thing is to please God.
>
> Whether he lives, or whether he dies . . . whether he is rich, or whether he is poor—whether he pleases man, or whether he gives offense—whether he is thought wise, or whether he is thought foolish—whether he gets blame, or whether he gets praise—whether he gets honour, or whether he gets shame—for all this the zealous man cares nothing at all. He burns for one thing; and that one thing is to please God, and to advance God's glory.[1]

The apostle Paul exemplified this godly zeal. He described his life ambition in 2 Corinthians 5:9: "So whether we are at home or away, we make it our aim to please [the Lord]."

Several years ago this became my favorite verse. One day I turned to it again, and my mouth dropped open when I discovered the next verse: "For we must all appear before the judgment seat of Christ, that each one may receive what is due him for the things done while in the body, whether good or bad" (2 Corinthians 5:10, NIV).

7 TAKE RESPONSIBILITY— BUT NOT TOO MUCH!

When I stand before the Judgment Seat of Christ, I will stand there alone, unable to point to the failings of others. God will not hold me accountable for what others have done, only for what I have done. At the judgment "every mouth [will] be stopped" (Romans 3:19). There will be no excuses. No self-justification. No blame-shifting. We are responsible to obey God regardless of what anybody else does.

In this chapter we will discuss the problems associated with taking too much or too little responsibility.

Don't Take Improper Responsibility . . .

God holds us responsible only for how we live *our* lives.

At times we may feel responsible for things that are not our responsibility. Perhaps we want to live other people's lives for them. I am guilty of this sometimes, and it leaves me either frustrated or angry. (It does not leave the person I am dealing with too happy either!)

If I told you that my goal is for it to rain tomorrow, you would think me foolish. What good is it to adopt goals outside of our control?

Few people make this mistake regarding the weather, but how often do people make it their goal for someone else to do something or to treat them a certain way?

Just as we cannot control the weather, we cannot control what anybody else does. We can control only what we do. It is presumptuous for us to adopt goals for others as if we were in control of what they do. Our goals must depend on our own behavior, therefore, not on what we hope others will do.

BLOCKED GOALS CAUSE FRUSTRATION

In the spring of 1991 my mother's parents were dying. Mom moved from Maryland into their house in Connecticut to try to make them happy during their last few months on earth. Unfortunately she could not make them happy, and she became very frustrated. She expressed her feelings to me one night on the phone. I suggested she check to make sure she was not adopting goals outside of her control.

"All you can do is all you can do, Mom," I told her. "You've got to be at peace with what's outside your control."

She called me back a few weeks later.

"I've made it my goal to do certain things for them," she said, "but it's no longer my goal for them to respond a certain way. As soon as I changed my goal, all that tension drained right out of me!"

I learned this principle from Larry Crabb's book *The Marriage Builder* (Zondervan, 1982). If you are married and have never read it, do yourself a favor and find a copy. It is one of the most helpful books I have ever read.

Michelle, the receptionist at the athletic club where I play racquetball, is an entrepreneur in homemade Christmas jewelry. Last November she set up her display on the front desk of the club. Sales were not going well, to put it mildly, and Michelle was not pleased.

"No one's buying my stuff," she said to me in disgust one afternoon as I signed in. "Yet they'll go to Foley's and buy the same thing for twice the price!"

"It sounds as if you're trying to control what others are doing instead of what you're doing," I responded. "I've made the same mistake many times. It can be awfully frustrating when we try to control something we can't control."

So Michelle began focusing on things she could do.

"You know," she said later, "when I wear the jewelry, it attracts attention, and sometimes that leads to sales. I think I'll wear something from the collection every day during the Christmas selling season. And maybe if I put the display over here. . . ."

Think back to a time you were frustrated or angry. Can you identify a goal you had that was blocked by somebody or something? Frustration and anger are almost always caused by blocked goals. A "blockable goal" is a goal that depends on someone or something else for its attainment. If our goal can be blocked, we have chosen the wrong goal! We should choose only unblockable goals—goals we can control.

This principle does not excuse us from taking legitimate responsibility. Rather, it frees us from taking illegitimate responsibility, enabling us to concentrate on the things we can control.

A friend and I worked for more than two years to create a tract that would present the Gospel in a warm and personal way. It was entitled "Searching for Satisfaction?" Before explaining the plan of salvation, we wanted to dwell long enough on God's wonderful character that the reader would *want* to know Him.

I was hoping the American Tract Society would publish the tract because I knew they would do a great job with distribution. When we presented the piece to the editor, however, he rejected it, explaining that ATS had decided to base its new tracts on current events, tapping into issues already on people's minds. Since our tract was not based on current events, he showed us the door.

Eight months later I decided to send the tract over the ATS editor's head to his boss, the publisher. I did so and the publisher liked it. But when the publisher brought it to the editor, he still did not want it. The publisher phoned me and said, "I don't know why he doesn't want to publish this. Although I'm his superior, I don't want to usurp his authority. This is normally his decision. Call me in seven days. I'll talk to him again about it and let you know what happens."

A week later I was dialing the phone, my heart pounding. I was so nervous I hung up before I finished dialing.

Why am I so nervous? I wondered. Then I realized my goal was for *them* to do something. I could not control what they did, even though I *really* wanted to. My goal, I decided, should be simply to inquire as to what they had decided. Immediately the nervousness went away.

When I made the call, the publisher responded, "I didn't talk to him again, but I had an idea. Our board of directors recently formed a new committee to review manuscripts. I've decided to send 'Searching for Satisfaction?' to that committee. If they like it, I'll be able to say to him, 'I think we need to go with this one.' Call me back in two weeks and I'll let you know what happens."

I wish I could tell you I learned my lesson the first time, but two weeks later I was so nervous while dialing that I hung up the phone. But again, when I corrected my goal, the nervousness disappeared immediately.

ATS eventually published the tract. That is the happy ending of the story, but not the point of it. I am learning to focus on what is under my control instead of wasting my time and energy focusing on what is not. As painful and drawn out as the experience was, I am glad I went through it.

This principle is helping me become bolder with others without pressuring them. This is especially helpful in witnessing.

Our goal should be to share Christ, not to get people to receive Christ. Their response is between them and God. If I am concerned with their response—something I cannot control—witnessing makes me nervous. If my goal is to get them to receive Christ, it also makes *them* nervous. They probably feel the way we all feel when dealing with a pushy salesperson. When salespeople adopt the wrong goal (trying to control what we do rather than what they do), they are manipulative rather than helpful. In witnessing, clarifying what is and is not our responsibility frees us up, and it also frees up the people to whom we witness. They can put their defenses down and think more clearly.

God wants us to speak with love, authority and boldness—without pressure. He says, "You shall speak my words to them, whether they hear or refuse to hear" (Ezekiel 2:7).

ONE WORTHY AMBITION

We should have one overriding goal in life: to please God. This is a goal that cannot be blocked. No person or circumstance can stop us from pleasing God, because regardless of what happens to us, we can still choose to respond in a way that pleases Him.

Since frustration and anger are caused by blocked goals, and since pleasing God is a goal that cannot be blocked, frustration and anger are red flags that tell us we have adopted the wrong goal. I want to please God with my life, so these red flags have become very helpful to me. They signal me to reexamine my goal. They warn me that I have gotten off course.

Let's say a pastor becomes frustrated by the number of church members who do not attend regularly. The red flag begins waving. He can waste his energy by focusing on what others should be doing, or he can focus on what *he* can do, and adopt the following mindset: *I can invite people to church. I can pray for them, visit them and prepare well. But I can't*

69

make them come. All I can do is all I can do. Fortunately I can still please God, regardless of what anybody else does.

. . . But Do Take Proper Responsibility

So far we have been talking about the danger of feeling responsible for things that are not our responsibility. A second danger is that we will fail to take responsibility for things that *are* our responsibility.

Think for a moment about the word itself. *Responsibility* means "response ability"—the ability to choose our own responses. If I say, "You make me so mad!" I am really saying, "You are controlling not only what *you* do, but also how I respond to you!" Put in those terms, my assertion is obviously ridiculous. I am denying that I have "response ability." I have deluded myself into thinking that you are controlling my responses. No wonder I feel like screaming!

We must not assume people have power over us that they really do not have. They are responsible to God for what they do, while we are responsible for our responses.

Someone told me about a mother who was deeply hurt when she learned that her daughter had eloped. The young woman, without her parents' knowledge or blessing, married a man much older than herself. Two weeks later the daughter invited her mother to lunch. The mother, afraid she would not be able to hide her feelings from her daughter, went to her pastor for advice. After counseling her, the pastor told her to feel free to use the sanctuary for prayer. As she prayed, the Lord showed her the power of Christ's blood to cleanse from all sin. Then He said to her, *You don't lose your peace over somebody else's sin, but only over your own.*

While we cannot control what others do or what happens to us, we can always control how we respond. Realizing this frees us to stop bemoaning bad circumstances or how others are mistreating us. We can focus instead on pleasing God, no matter what happens.

The mark of maturity is the realization that what happens to us is not nearly as important as how we respond to it.

Joseph experienced more adversity than most of us will ever face—sold into slavery by his own brothers, thrown into prison for a crime he did not commit and forgotten by Pharaoh's butler, who had promised to try to get him out of prison. Joseph could have had a victim's mindset and died a bitter old man, never fulfilling the awesome plans of God for his life. But Joseph had set his heart to please God. He did not justify unforgiveness in his own life by pointing to the magnitude of the sins committed against him. He forgave. He did not allow discouragement and self-pity to consume him. He acknowledged that his loving God was always with him, working behind the scenes to bring good out of bad situations. Because Joseph chose to please God in his responses, his problems became steppingstones rather than stumblingblocks.

When we meet adversity, let's not curse it, thinking it has the power to wreck our day—or our very lives. It has no such power. Rather, adversity provides opportunities for us to become more like the Lord Jesus Christ, who said, "I always do what is pleasing to [the Father]" (John 8:29).

Great people like Joseph are not those who have somehow managed to live lives without adversity. Great people are those who choose to please God regardless.

Understanding these responsibility issues can be extremely liberating, and it can help us prepare for the Day when we will not be able to hide behind any excuses. Hebrews 4:13 says: "Nothing in all creation is hidden from God's sight. Everything is uncovered and laid bare before the eyes of him to whom we must give account" (NIV).

8

THE FEAR OF MAN

O ne of the most common ways for us to get off course is to live for people's approval rather than God's approval. Proverbs 29:25 warns us that "the fear of man lays a snare." We are ensnared not only when we are afraid that people will hurt, humiliate or reject us, but also when we seek to impress others.

It is an easy trap to fall into. We become ensnared simply by entertaining the thought *What do people think of me?* It does not matter whether we conclude that people have bad thoughts about us or good thoughts. The bondage comes not from answering the question the wrong way; it comes from entertaining the question at all.

When I served as an academic advisor in a Christian university, a surprisingly high percentage of freshmen declared their intentions to go pre-med or pre-law. Obviously I could not discern the motives of any given individual. Some probably envisioned becoming doctors and lawyers because of their desire to help people, wishing to use their talents to please God and benefit others. Some, however, probably chose those majors because they sound impressive.

The fear of man contaminates decision-making. When we are choosing a career, for example, this fear would cause us to neglect thoughts like *What has God designed me to do?* and *How can I be of greatest benefit to other people?* Instead our thoughts would revolve around the question *Which career will make me look good?*

The fear of man is also a major cause of financial bondage. How easy it is to stretch beyond our price range to buy a more impressive house or car. Advertisers often appeal directly to this desire for status. A typical car commercial dramatizes the reactions we can expect from driving our new car. Our neighbors will stop their yardwork and stare admiringly. If the buyer is a man, his new car makes him irresistible to beautiful women, one of whom mysteriously appears in the passenger seat. But by the time we possess an impressive home and impressive car—wearing, of course, impressive clothes—we might be swimming in an impressive amount of red ink.

A college student dating a high school girl three years younger than himself sought advice. The age difference did not bother him, but his fraternity brothers were harassing him about it unmercifully. "We plan to get married one day," he said. "Ten years from now, who will care about a three-year age difference? The problem is not between my girlfriend and me. The problem is, my frat brothers won't stop tormenting me about it."

Actually, his real problem was not his fraternity brothers, but his fear of them. His fear was like a huge rubber band with one end looped around his waist and the other end pulled by his friends.

When we are experiencing pressure from peers, we can cut the rubber band by responding, "I'm living for God's approval, not yours."

God's Cure for Hypocrisy

At the Christian university where I used to teach, some of the students had adopted an unusual ritual. Around 10:30 on Sunday morning these students would get out of bed and hit the showers. The men would shave; the women would put on makeup and fix their hair. Then they put on their Sunday best and proceeded to the dining hall for lunch. Although they did not get up in time to go to church, it was obviously important to them to give that impression.

The Pharisees appeared righteous to men. They went about their good deeds such as fasting, praying and giving to the poor in such a way that others would notice. They were not trying to please God or benefit people; they were trying to impress people. Jesus spoke sharply to these Pharisees: "You are those who justify yourselves before men, but God knows your hearts; for what is exalted among men is an abomination in the sight of God" (Luke 16:15).

In the following passage Jesus warns that God will not reward *all* good deeds. God looks beyond each deed to the motive of the heart:

> "Beware of practicing your piety before men in order to be seen by them; for then you will have no reward from your Father who is in heaven. Thus, when you give alms, sound no trumpet before you, as the hypocrites do in the synagogues and in the streets, that they may be praised by men. Truly, I say to you, they have their reward."
>
> Matthew 6:1–2

Being seen by other people does not cause the forfeiture of eternal reward. Eternal reward is lost when a person does good deeds *in order to* be seen by men.

Some people give to the poor or to Christian work in order to help people and to serve God. They will receive eternal reward. But others give so that their generosity will be trumpeted publicly. Jesus says, "You have your reward." You have impressed man. Congratulations!

Understanding the Judgment Seat destroys any motivation to pretend we are something we are not. In Luke 12:1 Jesus warns us to "beware of the leaven of the Pharisees, which is hypocrisy." In the next two verses Jesus then provides God's cure for hypocrisy by revealing a very sobering truth about our future:

> "Nothing is covered up that will not be revealed, or hidden that will not be known. Whatever you have said in the dark shall be heard in the light, and what you have whispered in private rooms shall be proclaimed upon the housetops."
>
> verses 2–3

"Nothing is covered up that will not be revealed." I told my daughter, Jennifer, about this when she was six years old. A few weeks later I asked her if it had made any difference in her life. She pondered, then replied, "I don't think I lie very much anymore." When I asked her why not, she responded, "What's the use?"

The fear of God leads to integrity—even when no one is looking. Why lie, if God is the One who judges our hearts? Honesty and integrity are character traits of those who fear God.

Most dishonest people do not try to fool God; they simply fail to consider Him. They are more concerned about what other humans think than about what God thinks.

In *Knowing God* J. I. Packer wrote:

> I can hide my heart, and my past, and my future plans, from men, but I cannot hide anything from God. I can talk in a way that deceives my fellow-creatures as to what I really am, but nothing I say or do can deceive God. . . . He knows me as I really am, better indeed than I know myself. . . . Living becomes an awesome business when you realize that you spend every moment of your life in the sight and company of an omniscient, omnipresent Creator.[1]

If we look to man as our judge, then our judge is deceivable. Because humans judge by appearances, they can be fooled. Looking to them to judge breeds lies, hypocrisy and pretense.

Whom Do You Fear?

The fear of man played a major role in the Fall of man. In Eden "it was not Adam who was deceived, but the woman being quite deceived, fell into transgression" (1 Timothy 2:14, NASB). Why did Adam eat of the tree if he was not deceived, if he knew disobedience would bring death? Simply put, Adam wanted to please Eve.

When the curse fell on humankind, God said to Adam:

> "Because you have listened to the voice of your wife, and have eaten of the tree of which I commanded you, 'You shall not eat of it,' cursed is the ground because of you. . . ."
>
> Genesis 3:17

God held Adam responsible for allowing himself to be swayed away from God's will by another human being. God will hold us responsible, too. If He tells us to do one thing, and a person tells us (or even a thousand people tell us) to do something else, we are responsible to obey God rather than man. In the words of Thomas à Kempis, fifteenth-century devotional writer, "We should choose rather to have the whole world against us than to offend God."[2]

Jesus said that a special reward in heaven awaits those willing to bear rejection for His sake:

> "Blessed are you when men hate you, when they exclude you and insult you and reject your name as evil, because of the Son of Man. Rejoice in that day and leap for joy, because great is your reward in heaven. For that is how their fathers treated the prophets."
>
> Luke 6:22–23, NIV

Let's apply these words of Jesus to the following passage:

> Nevertheless many even of the authorities believed in [Christ], but for fear of the Pharisees they did not confess it,

76

lest they should be put out of the synagogue: for they loved
the praise of men more than the praise of God.

John 12:42–43

Jesus said, "Blessed are you when men hate you," but these
authorities were unwilling to be hated. Jesus said, "Blessed
are you when . . . they exclude you," but these authorities were
unwilling to be excluded.

God's prophets, on the other hand, loved the praise of God
more than the praise of men. They determined to please Him
regardless of the opinions of others. Their reward in heaven
is great. Similarly Jesus said that those rejected for His sake
will leap for joy if they simply see the truth about their reward
in heaven.

Jesus then issued this warning to those who live for the
praise of others: "Woe to you when all men speak well of you,
for that is how their fathers treated the false prophets" (Luke
6:26, NIV). The false prophets tailored their lives and mes-
sages to gain human approval.

SAUL'S DESIRE FOR HUMAN APPROVAL

To the extent that we are unwilling to be rejected by our
fellow human beings, we are in bondage to the fear of man.
King Saul, for example, catered to human approval and became a slave to his fear of rejection.

God commanded Saul not to allow the Israelites to take any
spoils from the city of Amalek after its overthrow. This command was, as you might imagine, exceedingly unpopular, so
Saul did not enforce the ban on gathering spoils. When confronted later by Samuel, the king eventually confessed to his
sin and to the root cause: "I have sinned . . . because I feared
the people and obeyed their voice" (1 Samuel 15:24).

Because Saul cared more about what the people thought
than about what God thought, God rejected him as king.

DANIEL'S UNYIELDING DEVOTION TO GOD

Another Old Testament character is exemplary in his freedom from the fear of man. Daniel lived for God's pleasure. He was on track to become second-in-command in Babylon, a highly respected and influential leader:

> Daniel became distinguished above all the other presidents and satraps, because an excellent spirit was in him; and the king planned to set him over the whole kingdom.
>
> Daniel 6:3

Driven by jealousy, the other leaders plotted against Daniel. They persuaded the king to sign a decree: Anyone offering a petition to any god or man except the king himself during the next thirty days would be thrown into the lions' den.

> When Daniel knew that the document had been signed, he went to his house where he had windows in his upper chamber open toward Jerusalem; and he got down upon his knees three times a day and prayed and gave thanks before his God, as he had done previously.
>
> verse 10

If Daniel feared man, he could easily have found justification for obeying the king's ordinance, concluding that preserving his life was a worthy goal. Alternatively Daniel could have disobeyed the decree in such a way that his disobedience could not be detected—praying without kneeling, for example, or in a more private place.

Even if Daniel had compromised by obeying the decree, his impact for God's Kingdom during his career may still have been substantial. But because he sought God's approval rather than man's, his impact was phenomenal.

After God delivered Daniel from the lions' den, the king made a decree:

> "That in all my royal dominion men tremble and fear before the God of Daniel, for he is the living God, enduring for ever;

his kingdom shall never be destroyed, and his dominion shall be to the end. He delivers and rescues, he works signs and wonders in heaven and on earth, he who has saved Daniel from the power of the lions."

verses 26–27

The Proper Response to False Accusation

Have you ever been falsely accused of something? As we learn to live for God's approval, we should expect to be accused falsely. Whereas the disclosure awaiting us at the Judgment Seat is bad news for the hypocrite, it is good news for the falsely accused. They welcome the disclosure of the truth.

The more we live for human approval, the more upset we will be by false accusation. Perhaps we have made the approval of others an idol. When falsely accused, we face a fork in the road. Either we will experience inner turmoil as we struggle to preserve our reputations, or we will be comforted by the knowledge that God is not deceived by man's lies.

Jesus Himself was accused of being a drunkard, a glutton, a bastard son and a demoniac. On one occasion some Jews asked Jesus, "Are we not right in saying that you are a Samaritan and have a demon?" (John 8:48). Jesus answered, "I have not a demon; but I honor my Father, and you dishonor me. Yet I do not seek my own glory; there is One who seeks it and *he will be the judge*" (verses 49–50, italics added).

When falsely accused, Jesus took comfort by focusing on the real Judge. "When he was reviled, he did not revile in return; when he suffered, he did not threaten; but he trusted to him who judges justly" (1 Peter 2:23).

Jesus also said:

> "If they have called the master of the house Beelzebul, how much more will they malign those of his household. So have no fear of them; *for nothing is covered that will not be revealed, or hidden that will not be known.*"

Matthew 10:25–26, italics added

Understanding the Judgment Seat can be comforting. We can know that "nothing is covered that will not be revealed." Human judgments endure for only a short time; God's judgments endure for eternity. At the Judgment Seat, false, worldly opinions will be abandoned. Everyone far and near will adopt God's opinion of us, because they will see the truth.

If we have been accused falsely because of our stand for Christ, there is cause for rejoicing. Jesus says,

> "Blessed are you when men revile you and persecute you and utter all kinds of evil against you falsely on my account. Rejoice and be glad, for your reward is great in heaven."
>
> Matthew 5:11–12

The promise of great reward produces great hope and joy.

God's Cure for Shame

If we live for human approval, we may find ourselves ashamed of what is right instead of what is wrong. This kind of shame diminishes not only our effectiveness in this life for the Kingdom, but also our rewards in the life to come. If we are ashamed of Christ before others, He will be ashamed of us at the Judgment Seat. "Whoever is ashamed of me and of my words in this adulterous and sinful generation," says Jesus, "of him will the Son of man also be ashamed, when he comes in the glory of his Father with the holy angels" (Mark 8:38).

God's cure for this kind of shame is revealed in a passage from John Bunyan's masterful allegory, *Pilgrim's Progress*. In this scene the character Faithful tells his friend Christian about being accosted by Shame, one of the enemy's craftiest agents:

> *Faithful:* Indeed this Shame was a bold villain. I could scarcely shake him out of my company. He haunted me and con-

tinually whispered to me about how unmanly it is to take religion seriously.

Christian: What did he say to you?

Faithful: He said, 'Twas a pitiful business for a man to mind religion; he said that a tender conscience was an unmanly thing; and that for a man to watch over his words and ways was to tie himself up from that liberty that the brave spirits of the times accustomed themselves to. He pointed out that only a few of the mighty, rich, or wise were Christians. None of them became Christians, in fact, until they were persuaded to be fools. He spoke of their Ignorance and their lack of understanding in all the natural sciences. He said that religion makes a man the ridicule of the times!

Christian: And what did you say to him?

Faithful: Say! I did not know what to say at first. The more I listened to him, the more the blood rushed to my face. I was almost overcome by Shame, but then I asked myself: Which is more important: what people think or what God thinks? And of course, I knew the answer to that! That which is highly esteemed among men is an abomination with God. Therefore, what God says to be best is best, though all the great men in the world be against it. God prefers a tender conscience; they that make themselves fools for the Kingdom of Heaven, are wisest; and the poor man that loves Christ, is richer than the greatest man in the world that hates him. "Shame, spiritual things are spiritually discerned, and I perceive that you are blind. Since God doth prefer us to believe Him rather than the idle speculations of so-called 'great' men, I will believe Him. I will gladly be called a fool by you, and wise by Him. Seeing that you are spiritually blind, your words have no weight with me. Shame, depart, you are my enemy; shall I entertain your thoughts rather than those of my Lord? How then shall I look Him in the face at his coming?"[3]

When we are accosted by Shame, we must do likewise. We must turn from what people think and focus on what God thinks. Isaiah 2:22 says, "Turn away from man in whose nostrils is breath, for of what account is he?"

One reason for the effectiveness of the apostle Paul was his turning away from people's opinions of him. "But with me," Paul writes, "it is a very small thing that I should be judged by you or by any human court. . . . It is the Lord who judges me" (1 Corinthians 4:3–4).

Ironically, as we learn to fear God rather than people, we experience a new freedom to love people. Can we genuinely love others when we are trying to impress them or when we are afraid of being rejected by them? Concern for our own reputations prevents us from wholeheartedly seeking their best interests. Only when we discard our selfish agendas are we free to truly love them.

To Please or Not to Please?

Is it right or wrong to try to please people? If our motive is to impress them or to avoid rejection, it is wrong. Paul confesses that previously he tried to please others out of wrong motives. He says in Galatians 1:10, "If I were still trying to please men, I would not be a servant of Christ" (NIV).

Trying to please people is right, on the other hand, if our motive is to benefit them. Paul also says, "I try to please all men in everything I do, not seeking my own advantage, but that of many, that they may be saved" (1 Corinthians 10:33).

Let's explore this paradox by examining the motives of two women who enjoy hosting large parties. In the eyes of their guests, both are outstanding hostesses, serving with grace and charm.

As the first woman finishes the preparations for her party, she determines to treat her guests the way she would like to be treated. She memorizes her guest list so she can greet each person by name. She resolves to introduce newcomers to the other guests so they will feel more comfortable. She hopes to encourage certain guests who are going through difficult times. When the doorbell rings, she opens the door and smiles.

The second woman memorizes her guest list to avoid the embarrassment of forgetting the name of an important guest. She frets about the marital discord between Bob and Janet, hoping they will not make a scene at her party. Early in the day she scolds her son about his messy bedroom, saying, "If our guests see your room like this, they'll think we're a bunch of slobs!" She makes a final pass through her house, scanning for the slightest defect. When the doorbell rings, she opens the door and smiles.

Both parties go well and both hostesses feel satisfied. The first, because her guests were honored; the second, because her reputation was enhanced. The first woman may be eligible for eternal reward; the second woman has her reward already.

In seeking eternal reward, we must train ourselves to fear God rather than man. The fear of God liberates; the fear of man ensnares. Our fear of people can keep us from acting in their best interests, as was the case with Eli, who feared his own sons (see 1 Samuel 2:22–36). God punished Eli "because his sons were blaspheming God, and he did not restrain them" (1 Samuel 3:13). God rebuked Eli with these words: "You honor your sons more than me" (1 Samuel 2:29, NIV).

On the other hand, because of Paul's liberty from the fear of man, he was amazingly bold even "in the face of great opposition" (1 Thessalonians 2:2). He kept doing what was in people's best interests, preaching the good news despite intense persecution. Paul shared the secret: "We are not trying to please men but God, who tests our hearts. . . . We were not looking for praise from men, not from you or anyone else" (1 Thessalonians 2:4, 6, NIV).

9

DEVELOPING A SERVANT'S HEART

Inside the door are peace of mind and consistent joy. Inside the door are kindness, thoughtfulness and fruitfulness. Those who live inside experience a richness of life most people have never dreamed possible. They become "rich in good deeds" (1 Timothy 6:18). They delight their Lord and Master. They are useful to Him. They will be great in His eternal Kingdom and close to Him forever.

What door could be so wonderful? It is the door of humility.

Unfortunately the concept of humility is often misunderstood. This was certainly the case in my life. Three months after committing my life to Jesus Christ as a high school student, I attended my first Christian camp and heard a well-meaning preacher say, "The road to humility is humiliation." Assuming he knew what he was talking about, and thinking I was now armed with a secret of spiritual growth, I pondered various self-humiliation techniques and came up with a method whereby I could debase myself in front of large numbers of people. I decided to pick up the trash in the school hallways during the high-traffic times between classes.

My peers watched in amazement. Occasionally I would be so embarrassed, I would skip a piece of trash. Then, feeling guilty, I would backtrack all the way down some long corridor just to pick up the piece I had missed.

I am happy to declare that God has a better way! The road to humility is not humiliation. When we are embarrassed, we think about ourselves more, not less. That is not real humility.

Before seeking to humble ourselves, it is a good idea to look first at God's instructions. If we belittle ourselves by dwelling on our shortcomings and failures, we may *seem* humble, but our minds are endlessly revolving around ourselves.

We are humble not when we debase ourselves, but when we lift our focus off of ourselves altogether. Real humility is not thinking less of ourselves; it is thinking of ourselves less. C. S. Lewis wrote:

> Do not imagine that if you meet a really humble man he will be what most people call "humble" nowadays: he will not be the sort of greasy, smarmy person who is always telling you that, of course, he is nobody. Probably all you will think about him is that he seemed a cheerful, intelligent chap who took a real interest in what *you* said to *him.* If you do dislike him, it will be because you feel a little envious of anyone who seems to enjoy life so easily. He will not be thinking about humility: he will not be thinking about himself at all.[1]

Adopting an outward focus is vital to our spiritual growth and fruitfulness. Certain problems cling to us when we focus on ourselves too much—problems such as anxiety, depression, boredom and loneliness. (We will look at how to conquer each of these in this chapter.) Preoccupation with self, regardless of the form it takes, is pride.

Pride encompasses much more than just feeling superior or arrogant. Pride is being wrapped up in ourselves. Some people are filled with themselves, thinking how incredible they are. Others are filled with themselves, thinking how pathetic they are. Some spend countless hours primping and staring admiringly in the mirror. Others stare at the mirror in disgust. But in all these cases, the mind is riveted on self.

When God told Moses to bring His people out of captivity, Moses responded, "Who am I, that I should go to Pharaoh and bring the Israelites out of Egypt? . . . I have never been eloquent. . . . O LORD, please send someone else to do it" (Exodus 3:11; 4:10, 13, NIV). Moses's response may sound humble, but the next verse says, "Then the LORD's anger burned against Moses" (verse 14, NIV). Why did God get angry? Let's take a closer look.

Moses was exalting himself in at least three ways. First, Moses responded as if he were smarter than God: *Lord, You probably don't realize this, but I have never been eloquent. I don't mean to be critical, but You've chosen the wrong guy. If You had come to me for advice, You'd know better than to ask what You're asking.*

Second, Moses was relying on himself and his own abilities. He put up objection after objection because he felt inadequate. And even though God tried to help him understand an important truth—*The point is not who you are, but that I will be with you*—Moses did not receive God's instruction. He continued to focus on his own inadequacy. Because he did not put his trust in God, fear dominated his heart.

Third, God wanted Moses to deliver two million people out of slavery. But Moses was not thinking about two million people. He was thinking about one person. That is not humility; it is pride in disguise. God wanted Moses to focus on those he was sent to help.

What Frees Us from Self-Centeredness?

So how do we free ourselves from self-absorption? Two ways: by casting our cares on the Lord and by focusing on the interests of others. Let's look at each of these in turn.

1. Casting Our Cares on the Lord

In 1 Peter God reveals the first way to get our focus off of ourselves—a passage that has changed my life. Someone pointed out to me once that two familiar verses in 1 Peter 5 express one continuous thought. In the first verse God commands us to humble ourselves, and in the second verse He tells us how to do it:

> [Verse 6] Humble yourselves, therefore, under the mighty hand of God, that He may exalt you at the proper time, [verse 7] casting all your anxiety upon Him, because He cares for you.
>
> 1 Peter 5:6–7, NASB

I had never realized pride and anxiety were connected. But it makes sense. When worries and cares are swirling around in our minds, we are wrapped up in our own little worlds. We cannot be sensitive to others because we are not thinking about others. God commands us, therefore, to correct our focus, to humble ourselves by casting our cares on Him. This breaks the fixation we have with ourselves and frees us to focus on God and others.

This was the secret of spiritual growth I had been seeking! It produced the first spiritual growth spurt of my life. Up until this time my mind had been a war. I suffered from so much turmoil and confusion I would sometimes say, "Lord, I need a vacation from my brain!" But when I began to cast my cares on Him, the effect was amazing: My mind and heart became peaceful. As I learned to cast my cares consistently, the turmoil ceased.

Through this one passage, 1 Peter 5:6–7, God blessed me not only with peace of mind but also with clarity of mind.

I should mention that during those first couple of years, I sometimes received an anxious thought that seemed "uncastable." I tried to cast it on the Lord, but it seemed to hit the ceiling and bounce back into my brain. This occurrence caused me to lose my peace, until the Lord showed me what was going on behind the scenes. Satan had thrown a flaming dart in my direction. The problem was no longer just the anxiety itself, but also a subtle lie I had received: *You can't cast this care on the Lord.* Obviously that thought contradicted God's command to cast "all" our cares on Him. Whatever God commands us to do, He enables us to do. When I recognized the lie and dismissed it as such, I was free once again to cast the care on the Lord.

One Sunday morning I was scheduled to speak in a large church. I had not spent much time in God's Word that week and felt guilty about it. I thought God might be saying to me, *Because you haven't been in My Word, let's see how you do on your own today, without My anointing. Maybe this experience will teach you a lesson.*

As I rehearsed the message in my mind, I thought, *This is going to be a disaster. I'm going to make a fool of myself!*

But God was not thinking what I feared He was thinking. He got through to me about thirty minutes before I left for the church. He said simply, *My son, cast all of your cares upon Me.* I let out a sigh of relief, and God's peace flooded in.

I share this story because of what happened next. My focus turned to those I was going to share with, and I began to think about how I might benefit them. My focus had been entirely on myself—until I cast my cares on the Lord.

It is important to recognize a danger associated with this teaching. A student might say, "This stuff about casting our cares is great! Lord, I have a major test on Friday and I put it in Your hands. I'm not going to study; I'm just going to trust You. You have all knowledge. It's a multiple choice test; it should be no problem for You. Just guide my hand, Lord."

Or a father might say, "The concept about casting our cares is wonderful! Lord, I put my family's finances in Your hands. I'm not going back to work. Matthew 6 says You feed the birds of the air, and they neither sow nor reap nor gather into barns. Me neither! Lord, I give You my responsibilities."

The Lord, of course, would say, "And I give them right back!" God has asked for our cares, not our responsibilities.

And make no mistake: His instruction about casting cares is not a suggestion. The God of the universe *commands* us to cast our cares on Him. Holding onto a care may seem a minor sin to us, but it is major to God. Notice the company this particular sin keeps in the following passage:

> "Take heed to yourselves, lest your hearts be weighed down with carousing, drunkenness, and cares of this life, and that Day come on you unexpectedly.... Watch therefore, and pray always that you may be counted worthy to ... stand before the Son of Man."
>
> Luke 21:34, 36, NKJV

Holding onto anxiety is the sin of an unsurrendered heart. God despises pride. The verse before the life-changing passage in 1 Peter says, "God opposes the proud, but gives grace to the humble" (1 Peter 5:5).

Let's be diligent, then, to obey God's command. Cares are not to be tolerated. As we look for Christ's return, we are urged to "be zealous to be found by him without spot or blemish, *and at peace*" (2 Peter 3:14, italics added).

"God, I'll Handle This One on My Own"

When my wife, Marcy, and I were in graduate school, a friend named Vicky knocked on the door of our apartment. As soon as we opened the door and invited her in, she burst into tears and began to share her worries about a probable breakup with her boyfriend. She was anxious about facing the future without him.

We invited Vicky to join us for lunch. After she finished her story, we encouraged her to cast her cares on the Lord. She did. Boyfriend or no boyfriend, she decided to put her future into the hands of a wise and loving Father. You could see the difference on her face. The Lord set her free.

She stayed for another hour or so, laughing and talking with us. When she started to leave, however, her countenance fell again. I asked her what thought had just entered her mind. She replied, "I just became afraid that the peace I have now won't last."

Do you see what the enemy was trying to do? Even before she left our apartment, he was saying to her, *Here, have another care.*

Cares indicate that we are not trusting God but are taking matters into our own hands. Because of His great love, God commands us to cast *all* our cares on Him—cares about our love life, work life, spiritual life, marriage, kids, finances, and future. Anxiety is never justified because anxiety is based on pride. We choose to be in control, to be "god" over the situation, to handle the matter on our own—as if we could do a better job running our lives than He could!

When We Have a Hard Time Trusting

When we have difficulty casting our cares on the Lord, finding it hard to relinquish control, the cause might be that we have not really believed the last part of 1 Peter 5:7: "He cares for you." He really does!

Some people believe God is so big that He is concerned only with the big picture—with galaxies, not with individual human beings. Their God is too small! In reality, God is *so* big that He knows us by name, and because of His great and intense love for us, He is concerned about everything that concerns us. No problem is too big or too small.

What a great One to have on our side! Nothing ever fazes or intimidates God. He always understands the problem and knows how to fix it. He is excellent at bringing good out of bad situations. Furthermore He is always there for us, always faithful. We sometimes turn our backs on Him, but He never turns His back on us.

So why not trust Him? Why not rest our heads on His chest? He welcomes us there. He wants us "to cleave to Him" (Joshua 22:5).

If we fear God's will in an area, we will not entrust that area to Him. Lack of trust grieves God and greatly hinders our growth in Christ. Behind the lack of trust is a lie that denies God's goodness. The truth is, God is much more concerned about our happiness and fulfillment than we will ever be. He wants what is best for us.

Sometimes we pray about a care, but the anxiety remains. Often this happens when we are asking God to fulfill our own agendas, and we fear He will not give us what we want ("My kingdom come, my will be done. . ."). When we put something into God's hands, we must acknowledge His goodness. We may not get our agenda, but that is O.K. If His is different, it is because His is better.

Hannah Whitall Smith wrote:

> He is our Father, and He loves us, and He knows just what is best, and therefore, of course, His will is the very most blessed thing that can come to us under any circumstances. I do not understand how it is that the eyes of so many Christians have been blinded to this fact. But it would really seem as if God's own children were more afraid of His will than of anything else in life—His lovely, lovable will, which only means loving-kindnesses and tender mercies, and blessings unspeakable to their souls. I wish only that I could show to everyone the unfathomable sweetness of the will of God. Heaven is a place of infinite bliss because His will is perfectly done there, and our lives share in this bliss just in proportion as His will is perfectly done in them. He loves us—loves us, I say—and the will of love is always blessing for its loved one.[2]

As we meditate on the truth about what God is like, our trust grows and we become *delighted* to put our anxieties—and ourselves—in His hands.

2. Focusing on the Interests of Others

The second way we free ourselves from self-centeredness is by focusing on the needs of others. When we serve God by helping others, we discover the secret of life! Jesus says that "he who loses his life for my sake will find it" (Matthew 10:39). We discover life as God intended it.

A physician I heard about gave up a successful practice in California to become a medical missionary in Africa. Behind his back, some of his associates expressed their opinion that his decision was unbelievably foolish. When he got wind of their sentiments in a letter from a friend, he wrote back, "Tell them I've finally discovered what it means to really live."

In his book *The Kingdom of God Is a Party,* Anthony Campolo relates an incident that occurred when he traveled to Hawaii to speak at a Christian conference. Because Tony had crossed so many time zones to get there from his home in Pennsylvania, his internal clock was off kilter. At 3:30 one morning he wandered the streets of Honolulu looking for a place that would serve breakfast. He finally found a little diner still open. He took a seat and ordered.

Suddenly a group of women burst in and sat down. He could tell, by how they were dressed and what they said, that they were prostitutes. Tony overheard one woman tell the others that her birthday was the next day. The women responded sarcastically, accusing her of trying to get attention. But after the women left, Tony asked the man behind the counter if he knew the woman's name. Then he made preparations, hoping she would return around the same time the next morning.

She did, and was shocked to find a personalized birthday cake, the diner decorated in her honor and a roomful of prostitutes who had heard about the party.

As Tony led the women in singing happy birthday, tears began to run down the woman's cheeks. As it turned out, she had never had a birthday cake, and no one had ever sung happy birthday to her in her whole life.[3]

This story inspires me. I want to be a person God uses. I want my life to be a fountain of blessing to others. I dare say this woman took a step closer to the Kingdom of God that day.

What caused Tony Campolo to see this opportunity? What was going on in his mind? I suspect he had spent time meditating on verses that challenge us to break out of self-preoccupation.

If we want to become extraordinarily loving people, the Scripture talks about several ways to develop the mindset of a servant. We will take a look at three.

Love Your Neighbor as Yourself

Sometimes I do not feel like loving the poor, the hurting or the unsaved. How can I get the motivation I need to reach out to them? Should I try to motivate myself by feeling guilty?

God's way is different—and much more effective. The motivation we need comes from obeying these words: "You shall love your neighbor as yourself" (Mark 12:31).[4] Jesus illustrated this principle with the story of the Good Samaritan.

Did Jesus say the Samaritan was motivated by feelings of love to help the wounded man? On the contrary, Jesus had already disclosed the Samaritan's secret: He loved his neighbor *as himself.* In other words, he thought, *If I had been beaten and robbed, and if I were lying half-dead in the street, what would I want someone to do for me?* His motivation to help came from the mindset he had chosen to adopt. The two who passed the wounded man before the Samaritan arrived could have helped him, but they failed to put themselves in his shoes.

The same principle is found in Hebrews 13:3, a verse that exhorts us to care for prisoners and for the physically abused—two groups of people who are easy to neglect: "Remember those who are in prison, *as though in prison with them. . ."* (Hebrews 13:3, italics added). This verse does not compel me to think, *I should do something nice for those in prison,* but rather, *If I were in prison, what would I want someone to do for me?*

Hebrews 13:3 goes on to say, "And [remember] those who are ill-treated, *since you also are in the body*" (italics added). Again, to obey this verse I must consider, *If it were my body getting beaten up, what would I want someone to do for me?*

In the same way, to be motivated for evangelism, we do not need to wait for a feeling of compassion for the lost; we must simply love our neighbor as ourselves. If I hear that a thousand people will die and go to hell tomorrow, I may feel unmoved. My tendency is to neglect non-Christians because of my busy schedule. But how would I feel if one of those thousand was me? How diligent would I want Christians to be in their outreach to me? I would want someone to go to the ends of the earth. "So whatever you wish that men would do to you," said Jesus, "do so to them" (Matthew 7:12).

Serve the Lord by Serving Others

A second way to become a loving person with a servant's heart is illustrated by a story from Edith Schaeffer.

During the Great Depression, a number of unemployed men rode the rails from town to town looking for employment. Often they hid in empty freight cars or under the train itself. Periodically these hobos would hop off the train and knock on the back doors of houses to ask for something to eat.

Edith and Francis Schaeffer lived near some railroad tracks. Edith was amazed at how many men came to their house asking for food. Years later she discovered that their home had been marked, along with other homes near the rail lines, as one that would show compassion.

When one of these men headed toward their back door, Edith would not think, *Oh, no. There's another one! With all I have to do today. . . .* Instead her heart would leap for joy as she began to prepare a tray of food.

> I would butter the bread, cut a lovely big tomato in even slices and pepper them, place them on the bread, and then decide to add bacon. I would sizzle one slice to fold over the

94

tomato and add two leaves of lettuce. For a second sandwich I'd prepare him my own favorite: walnut halves stuck into the butter, salted on one slice, and then the second piece of buttered bread placed on top. Now for the steaming hot soup. . . .[5]

Edith's children would help her fix a bouquet of flowers in an ivy leaf to decorate the tray. (Her daughter would ask, "What'll he *think* of all that, Mummy?") Finally Edith would put a gospel of John next to the flowers and bring it all out to the man on the back porch. "Please read this. It really is very important."

The men, as you might imagine, were shocked. They would mumble something like, "Is all this for me, ma'am?" Can you imagine the impact these simple acts of kindness had on all these men? Many had never been treated that way in their lives. Edith Schaeffer's kindness helped prepare the soil of their hearts for the Gospel.

But good works like this do not just happen. They come from a specific mindset that Edith had chosen to adopt. What motivated her to look to their interests?

First, Hebrews 13:2: "Do not neglect to show hospitality to strangers, for thereby some have entertained angels unawares." Edith thought, *How would I want to treat this person if he were an angel? He might actually be one!*

A second Scripture also contributed to Edith's mindset:

"I was hungry and you gave me something to eat, I was thirsty and you gave me something to drink, I was a stranger and you invited me in, I needed clothes and you clothed me, I was sick and you looked after me, I was in prison and you came to visit me. . . . I tell you the truth, whatever you did for one of the least of these brothers of mine, you did for me."

Matthew 25:35–36, 40, NIV

Edith thought, *How would I want to treat this person if he were the Lord Jesus Himself?*

What we do for "one of the least of these," whether good or bad, is accepted by the Lord as having been done unto Him.

This was the very passage that captivated the heart of Mother Teresa. In *Words to Love By* she wrote:

> At the end of our lives, we will not be judged by how many diplomas we have received, how much money we have made or how many great things we have done. We will be judged by "I was hungry and you gave me to eat. I was naked and you clothed me. I was homeless and you took me in." . . . This is Christ in distressing disguise.[6]

Count Others More Important Than Yourself

A third way to develop a servant's heart is revealed in Philippians 2, where God offers another key to unlock the prison of pride. But first we must recognize *when* we are proud. God says we are proud whenever we go through our day without considering the interests of other people!

> With humility of mind let each of you regard one another as more important than himself; do not merely look out for your own personal interests, but also for the interests of others.
>
> Philippians 2:3–4, NASB

What is our mindset on days when we pursue only our own interests? When we serve only ourselves, we are subconsciously considering ourselves more important than everyone else. We do not have to *feel* proud to be proud. We do not have to feel superior to other people to be proud. We exalt ourselves by preoccupation with ourselves and our own interests. God commands us, therefore, to humble ourselves.

I do not know about you, but if I do not intentionally humble myself in accordance with what God says—by casting my cares on the Lord and by focusing on the interests of others—I default to self-centered living. I become filled with thoughts of what I want and when I want it, and I pursue my own interests all the time.

When I miss opportunities God is giving me to love people, it is not because I shout, "No, I won't do it!" Too often I simply do not notice the interests of anyone else because I am so wrapped up in myself. Philippians 2:3–4 is an invitation out of self-centeredness.

As you look at this passage, examine yourself. Do not ask, *Am I familiar with these verses?* or *Have I heard this before?* Rather, ask yourself, *Am I doing this? Am I obeying these verses? Do I regard others as more important than myself? Do I look out for their interests?* If we meditate on these verses and apply them daily, we will become rich in good deeds and rich toward God. A servant's heart is precious in God's sight. It is the secret to greatness in God's Kingdom (see Mark 10:43) and to being close to God's throne forever (see Mark 10:37–45).

At the Judgment Seat, I fear many will hear God say, "My child, for years you asked Me to bless your marriage, but you never let go of your pride. Your thoughts revolved around what *you* wanted and around what your spouse should be doing for *you.* You didn't humble yourself, as I instructed you to do. You didn't count your spouse as more important than yourself. Had you done so, I would have poured life and blessing into your marriage."

Many others may hear God say, "My child, for years you asked Me to bless your business, but you never let go of your pride. You didn't count your customers and co-workers as more important than yourself. Had you done so, I would have blessed you in your business."

I first applied Philippians 2:3–4 about twenty years ago. The bad news is, my obedience lasted only about a week. The good news is, I had one of the best weeks of my life! God was using me, and I had incredible joy showing His kindness to people.

Why did I stop? Frankly, I cannot remember. I guess I just got my mind on other things and returned to my "default position" of self-centeredness.

But I got back on track a year or two later—for about another week. In fact, for about fifteen years I put in a few weeks of quality service annually. Then God revealed to me that my life would not be what He wanted it to be until I made it my regular practice to count others more important than myself.

Although it is still easy to become self-preoccupied, two helpful exercises now remind me to get into "servant mode" several times a day.

First, in my daily thanksgiving times, I count my wife, my kids and my students as more important than myself. When I pray for my wife, for instance, I say, "Lord Jesus, please live through me today to be the kind of husband who would delight the Father's heart, who would treat Marcy the way You want her to be treated, who would love her, serve her, cherish her and count her as more important than myself." Then I take a moment to count my wife as more important than myself. I go through the same process with my children. I cannot tell you how much this little exercise has enriched my relationships with Marcy and the kids!

Second, whenever my phone rings, I take a few seconds before I pick up the phone to count the caller as more important than myself. This exercise brings the passage to mind several times a day.

Larry Crabb writes about a practice he has adopted to cultivate a servant's heart:

> When the idea first became clear to me that every word I utter should be governed by the motive of ministry, I struggled to build a new mental tape library. When I arrived home from work every evening, I remained in my car for a few minutes and repeated to myself, "My goal as I walk through the front door is to minister to my family. I sure hope I'm greeted by a happy wife, delightful kids, and a working refrigerator, but no matter what I discover inside, my purpose is to minister in love to my family."
>
> For many men, there are few moments more fearful than returning home after a day's work. As they stumble wearily through the front door, their mental tape recorders often play

words like "I hope the hamster didn't fall in the toilet again" or "If my wife gripes about her day after the one I've just had, I think I'll walk out." Thoughts of this sort tempt husbands to wrap themselves in protective layers of bored silence, cold retreat, or absorption in the TV or newspaper.

Self-protective manipulation comes naturally; servant-like ministry doesn't. The attitude of ministry requires careful cultivation. [We must] diligently attend to our thinking and choose to adopt the goal of ministry.[7]

Just as we control what we look at in the physical realm, we also control whose interests we look to. Paul indicated that this outward focus was the reason Timothy was so valuable in God's service:

I hope in the Lord Jesus to send Timothy to you soon. . . . I have no one like him, who will be genuinely anxious for your welfare. They all look after their own interests, not those of Jesus Christ. But Timothy's worth you know. . . .

Philippians 2:19–22

Like Timothy, Job was also used by God to bless many people, because Job humbled himself and looked to the interests of others:

"I delivered the poor who cried, and the fatherless who had none to help him. The blessing of him who was about to perish came upon me, and I caused the widow's heart to sing for joy. . . . I was eyes to the blind, and feet to the lame. I was a father to the poor, and I searched out the cause of him whom I did not know. I broke the fangs of the unrighteous, and made him drop his prey from his teeth."

Job 29:12–13, 15–17

Wouldn't you love to know a person like this? Wouldn't you love to *be* a person like this?

But if we do not regard others as more important than ourselves, any service we provide is likely to be begrudging, resentful and joyless. When we count others as more important than ourselves, however, we *want* to bless them. Serving them is a delight. We love to serve. We live to serve.

A friend asked me once to counsel with him and his wife because they were having severe marital difficulties. She no longer wanted help; she wanted a divorce. To prove to me that the situation was hopeless, she told me, "I just don't love my husband anymore." Case closed.

It seemed to me, however, that she did not understand what love is. If love is just a feeling, then no marriages would last. But love is a decision—to count another person as more important than ourselves, to focus on that person's interests, to treat him or her the way we would like to be treated. Loving feelings follow *after* such a decision is made.

Nor is this decision a one-time choice. Love is a decision we have to make thousands of times—until it becomes our mindset. "Let this mind be in you, which was also in Christ Jesus" (Philippians 2:5, KJV). If Jesus had looked only to His own interests, He would probably never have come down from heaven. He certainly would not have gone to the cross. But He looked to *our* interests because He chose to count us as more important than Himself! Nor did Jesus suddenly adopt this mindset on the day He was crucified. Before His crucifixion He stooped down and washed the feet of His disciples (see John 13:3–17). After His resurrection He made them breakfast (see John 21:9–14). He spent every day counting others more important than Himself.

Humility Helps Dispel the Gloom

If we want to follow Jesus, we must adopt the same mentality. We are thus released from self-centeredness and from the many problems associated with it.

A mindset of humility helps to dispel not only anxiety, as we have seen, but also the gloom of depression, boredom and loneliness.

DISPELLING THE GLOOM OF DEPRESSION

A young man visited a pastor in Dallas several years ago. Depression had gripped him for nine months. As he shared his story, the pastor listened intently. Afterward he offered no counsel. Instead he simply thanked the young man for sharing and asked him a favor. Writing a name and a hospital room number on a piece of paper, the pastor said, "This person has *got* to be visited today, but my schedule is so tight, I can't do it. Would you stop on your way home and make the visit for me?" The young man was surprised, but he consented and headed toward the hospital.

Something amazing happened in the next hour. As he visited with the sick person, the power of his depression was broken. He emerged from the gloom that had plagued him for nine months. Why? Because he finally focused on somebody other than himself.

This is not to say that every case of depression can be resolved this way. Some depression is physiological in origin, caused by chemical imbalance. Most depression, however, grips us simply because we adopt the wrong focus. The pastor in Dallas had learned a secret from the Lord Jesus Himself: Joy comes from loving others—from getting our focus off of ourselves and asking, "How can I be a blessing? How can I help somebody else? How can I give my life away?"

Please read Jesus' words very carefully:

> "These things I have spoken to you, that my joy may be in you, and that your joy may be full. This is my commandment, that you love one another as I have loved you."
>
> John 15:11–12

Hebrews 1:9 says Jesus had "the oil of joy" above His companions (NIV). Jesus had more joy than anybody else because He loved more than anybody else.[8]

When I am depressed, my attention is on me. My feelings. My problems. I am the center of my world. At those times I have learned to ask myself, *Are you loving anyone else? Are you caring for anyone else?* The answer is always the same: *No. I'm trying to figure out why I'm so depressed.* As soon as I turn outward to truly care for someone else, the depression lifts and God's joy takes its place. God did not create us to live for ourselves, and we are miserable as long as we do. The more I give myself away, the more I walk in joy.

Dr. Karl Menninger, the famous psychiatrist, once gave a lecture on mental health and was answering questions from the audience. "What would you advise a person to do," asked one man, "if that person felt a nervous breakdown coming on?"

Most people expected him to reply: "Consult a psychiatrist." To their astonishment, he replied: "Lock up your house, go across the railway tracks, find someone in need and do something to help that person."[9]

God says, "If you pour yourself out for the hungry and satisfy the desire of the afflicted, then shall your light rise in the darkness and your gloom be as the noonday" (Isaiah 58:10). What a wonderful picture of what happens in our hearts when we turn outward to care for others!

Have you ever been outside in the early morning when a fog hangs over the landscape? Have you seen the morning sun come over the horizon and burn away that gloom? This is what happens in our hearts, except it is not the morning sun burning away the gloom; it is the *noonday* sun.

DISPELLING THE GLOOM OF BOREDOM

I once found myself frantically flipping through the television channels, trying desperately to find something to alleviate my boredom. To my dismay, the best show I could find was bowling. (I hate bowling!)

My real problem was not the pitiful selection of programs on TV, but preoccupation with myself. When I am bored, I am focusing on the fact that I am not having a good time. Concerned only about my own interests, I search for something or someone to entertain me. My problem is multiplied if I try to fill the emptiness with various self-indulgences. Whenever I seek only my own happiness and fulfillment, I discover just how awful life can be.

God has called you and me to a higher purpose: to live with the same mindset as the One who "came not to be served but to serve" (Matthew 20:28). When I am bored, the opposite is true of me. I am seeking not to serve, but to be served. I am here to be entertained.

God calls us to a complete change in orientation. To free ourselves from boredom, we must begin to love and serve others. Only then do we discover a life of purpose, adventure and significance. And as God uses us to build His Kingdom, boredom becomes a thing of the past.

Dispelling the Gloom of Loneliness

A few summers ago I struggled with intense loneliness. My job situation had changed so that I was working by myself instead of with a staff. Oppressive loneliness settled on me every morning for several weeks. Each day I would thank God for His blessings, and the gloom would lift, providing temporary relief. The next morning, however, it always returned. My mind was dominated by a single thought: *How can I get rid of this loneliness?*

Loneliness makes it difficult to establish friendships or even to reach out to existing friends. C. S. Lewis calls lonely people those "who simply want friends and can never make any."

When you were a kid, did you ever use a magnet to chase around other magnets? The more desperate a lonely person is for companionship, the more others tend to avoid that person. If I am lonely and reach out to others, the problem is that I have the wrong goal. I am not really loving them; I am trying to get them to love me. To be blunt, I am trying to use them to meet my own need, and people do not like to be used.

After about three weeks of this torture, I suddenly realized I was not caring for anybody else in the world. I had become the center of my universe. My goal in life was to get rid of my pain. At that moment I made a decision to begin caring for others. The loneliness disappeared, and this time it did not come back.

When we humble ourselves in this way, we are like a magnet that has been "turned around." Instead of avoiding us, people are attracted to us. People hate to be used but they love to be loved. They love to be listened to, to be encouraged, to have others show genuine interest in what is happening in their lives.

Samuel Shoemaker, an evangelical leader after World War II, observed that "we are lonely not because we are not loved but because we do not love."[10] Someone has said, "You can make more friends in two months by being interested in other people than you can in two years by trying to get other people interested in you."

When struggling with loneliness, we may feel like an empty cup in need of filling. At those times we need to admit something that we may not *feel* is true: God loves us. Our need for love is already met in Christ. We need to meditate on this, to affirm its truth continually. Once this realization gets down into our hearts, our perspective changes. We begin to take on a "full cup" perspective. We realize we have something to give people. And thus we experience the reality of 1 John 4:19: "We love, because he first loved us."

Over the last few years my loneliness has tried to come back several times. As I drive to campus on a gloomy day, sometimes my mood begins to match the weather. As soon as I recognize what is happening, however, I say to myself, *I'm not going down this path again! I need to get back to a servant mindset. Whom can I serve? Can I give a student a ride to class? How can I be helpful to somebody?* As I seek to be a blessing, the loneliness disappears.

Humility on the Job

Recently I heard a message given by Christian philosopher Dr. Arthur Holmes on why God created work as part of His design. If we work just to make a living, Dr. Holmes contended, we have missed the point and our work is likely to be unsatisfying as a result. Work, according to Dr. Holmes, is an opportunity to serve others.

His talk reminded me of the experiences of two friends of mine.

Mike Shrock is a friend from my college days. Mike owns a landscaping business in Oregon called Living Color Landscaping. When he first took over the business, it included landscaping on fourteen Burger King franchises. From the outset Mike saw his business as a ministry and really put his heart in his work. He even went to Disneyland to study how they did their landscaping. Mike's goal was to help franchise owners by making the landscaping so sharp and colorful that it would grab the attention of people driving by. If Mike learned from an owner that his franchise was about to be inspected, he would send out an extra crew to plant new flowers and re-mow the lawn (even if it had been mown just a few days earlier) to make the place look spectacular.

Needless to say, his customers were thrilled with the service they received, and Mike's company grew to handle 48 Burger King accounts, along with many others. Mike took much joy in his work.

About two years ago Mike, who loves to pastor, became the co-pastor of a small church. He decided not to draw a salary from the church, but to keep his landscaping business as a source of income. He began to see his job as God's provision. It provided the finances to pay the bills so Mike could pastor the church.

But this change in the way he viewed his landscaping job brought an unintended consequence. As he labored just to make a buck, he became extremely bored.

"To be honest with you," Mike told me at one point, "for about a year now I've hated my job. Nowadays I find myself checking the contracts to make sure we're doing what we said we would do. I *never* used to check the contracts—because we were always going so far beyond what we said we would do."

When Mike realized recently that he was *using* his customers rather than serving them, he corrected his mindset.

"Instead of focusing on how bored I am," Mike says, "I look for something else I can do to make their place look better. It's really made my landscaping work a joy again."

Then there is James Tennison, a friend who makes his living painting portraits and teaching art at a local university. James paints beautiful portraits, but about five years ago he struggled with a bad attitude because he wanted to paint other things. Landscapes, for instance. But landscapes do not pay the bills. So James painted portrait after portrait.

"I used to hate doing portraits," James says. "I secretly hoped every one would be my last. I used to wish for an inheritance so I could paint what I want."

Fortunately God did a great work in James' heart. This artist began to see his work as an opportunity to serve. He humbled himself. As an act of love, he began to count his clients as more important than himself. The results were dramatic.

"The servant mindset changed everything," he says. "Rather than dwelling on myself and my desire to do my own thing, I began focusing on my clients and on how much joy I would bring them if I did a wonderful painting of a child or spouse."

Portrait painting is not just a job for him anymore; it is a ministry. James often mentions how much joy he now has in his work.

This change in approach also helped his teaching. James used to get nervous when he had to do painting demonstrations at the university. After all, he was supposed to be the expert. His students were watching. What if he blew it? What if he painted something and it looked stupid?

"I finally realized, This isn't about *me;* this is about *them,*" he says. "I'm here to serve them. The nervousness has disappeared."

Humility Cures Stage Fright

As we can see from James' experience at the university, humility cures yet another problem associated with a self-centered focus: stage fright. If we stand up to speak or sing God's Word, and stage fright transforms us into nervous wrecks, God's Kingdom is hindered. Stage fright can diminish or even destroy our effectiveness.

I have been a nervous wreck on several occasions. Nasty symptoms arise when I am plagued by nervousness: I fail to establish rapport with my audience, I talk too fast, my mind goes blank and my jokes are not funny. These nervous symptoms short-circuit the communication process. Fortunately God has a cure.

The nervousness associated with stage fright is caused by having the wrong goal. I am seeking either to impress others or to avoid humiliation, especially in front of large numbers of people. (Tape recorders and videocameras make me even more nervous because then I can make a fool of myself and have the moment immortalized on tape!) If I seek to impress or to avoid humiliation, I am focusing not on the interests of my audience, but on my own interests. I am not trying to advance God's Kingdom, but my own.

The cure? There is only one: I must change my goal. I must lay down my own reputation and seek to benefit those I am sharing with. "The goal of our instruction," Paul wrote, "is love from a pure heart" (1 Timothy 1:5, NASB). God is calling us to purity of heart, purity of motive.

A youth minister told me recently he never gets nervous when he talks to his youth group, but he often gets nervous when he talks to their parents. "Now I realize why," he said. "I am trying to help the kids, but trying to impress the parents."

Paul says, "You yourselves know how I lived among you . . . serving the Lord with all humility" (Acts 20:18–19). Paul's humility manifested itself in his public speaking. He goes on to say, "I did not shrink from declaring to you anything that was *profitable*" (Acts 20:20, italics added). Paul did not shrink back, because he was not thinking about himself. He was thinking about how to profit those with whom he was sharing.

Here, then, is the essence of what God has been teaching me about humility in public speaking: *Make love your goal. Concentrate on the individuals with needs, on how you can help them, on how you can best love them. And in this way you will be pleasing in God's sight.*

It is wonderful! When I correct my focus, the nervousness always disappears. There have been no exceptions. Why? Because unlike taking three deep breaths, listening to tapes of ocean noises or other methods to reduce nervousness, this method puts the ax to the root of the problem. Because nervousness is caused by having the wrong goal, we must change our goal in order to cure it. Indeed, nervousness disappears when we shift our goal from impressing others to serving them.

The issue is not whether we can avoid the uncomfortable feelings associated with stage fright. There is a much more important issue: Will we allow God's Kingdom to flow through us into the lives of other people?

If we want to be people God can use, we must walk through the door of humility. If our secret motive is to exalt ourselves, the Holy Spirit wants no part of it. If our motive is to benefit people, on the other hand, then the Holy Spirit will help our preparation and our presentation as well.

At the Judgment Seat of Christ everyone's motives will be revealed. It should be an interesting day!

10 STAY OUT OF HIS CHAIR!

W e have been talking about the self-centeredness of pride. Pride is also evident when we take on jobs God reserves exclusively for Himself. Jack Taylor says, "If you want to get along with God, stay out of His chair!"

In this chapter let's look at four ways people exalt themselves into God's place.

We Exalt Ourselves When We Seek Revenge

Forgiving others is sometimes difficult because we want justice to be done. We want to even the score. In a word, we want revenge. Revenge can be subtle. It need not manifest itself in some horrible act of violence. It might show up by our giving someone the silent treatment, or by our refusing to establish eye contact, or by our demonstrating passivity in a relationship, not expending the energy to treat the other person well.

Although we may feel justified in our attempts to pay people back for wrongs they have done, the fact is, vengeance is not our job. Romans 12:19 says, "Beloved, never avenge yourselves, but leave it to the wrath of God; for it is written, 'Vengeance is mine, I will repay, says the Lord.'"

If anyone had good cause (and good opportunity!) to get revenge, it was Joseph. His brothers were so jealous of him as a boy that they decided to kill him. But as they were about to carry out their plans, an interesting opportunity presented itself. Some slave traders were passing by, and Joseph's brothers saw their chance not only to get rid of Joseph forever but to make a little money in the process. So they sold him into Egyptian slavery.

Many years later, after Joseph became the second most powerful man in Egypt, his brothers feared his vengeance (Genesis 50:15, 18–21):

> They said, "It may be that Joseph will hate us and pay us back for all the evil which we did to him." . . . His brothers also came and fell down before him, and said, "Behold, we are your servants." But Joseph said to them, "Fear not, for am I in the place of God?"

What a fascinating response! Joseph saw the issue clearly. He trusted in the God "who judges justly" (1 Peter 2:23). Vengeance, Joseph knew, is something God reserves for Himself. He dared not exalt himself into God's place.

We Exalt Ourselves When We Judge Others

Imagine that I am visiting the president of a major corporation, and during our conversation I begin to criticize his executive secretary. He might listen for a few minutes, wondering where I am going with this. But eventually he will probably say something like, "Who do you think you are?!"

When we pass judgment on someone, the Bible asks a similar question: "Who are you to pass judgment on the servant

110

of another? It is before his own master that he stands or falls" (Romans 14:4).

When I accept a judgmental thought about someone, my heart becomes hardened toward that person. The Holy Spirit convicts me that I have no right to pass judgment on the servant of another. That person is not accountable to me. I am exalting myself, looking down coldly from the judge's bench.

When I decide to leave the judging to God, on the other hand, my heart softens. I see the person with fresh eyes, and God's kindness begins to flow through me once again. When I give up my judging of others, I am not saying my judgments are always inaccurate; I am simply admitting that judging is not my job.

Paul writes, "Why do you pass judgment on your brother? Or you, why do you despise your brother? For we shall all stand before the judgment seat of God . . . Each of us shall give account of himself to God" (Romans 14:10, 12).

I think the Lord is saying two things in this passage. "First," He says, "you need not judge your brother, because *I* am going to judge your brother. Second, be careful how you think about your brother, because I am going to judge you, too!"

James writes, "Establish your hearts, for the coming of the Lord is at hand. Do not grumble, brethren, against one another, that you may not be judged; behold, the Judge is standing at the doors" (James 5:8–9).

We Exalt Ourselves When We Judge God Himself

Pam Moore, once the traveling companion of Corrie ten Boom, recounts the following story:

> A young woman came to see me on two occasions. In our conversations she twice referred to God's treatment of her as "cruel." She was in her late twenties and upset about still being single.

Rising in my heart when she used the word *cruel* was a terrific indignation and also a sadness. She did not understand God's character. I told myself that I must not allow her to blaspheme God a third time. I felt afraid for her because one day we will be accountable before God for every word we have spoken.

In God's plan I was 42 before God brought my husband, Carey, to me. We have been given the happy marriage I had always dreamed of, and I thank God for being so good and kind. But even if God had not had marriage in His plan for me, He would *still* be good and kind. God is *always* good and kind.[1]

In learning to wait patiently for a husband, Pam was resting in the fact that God is good and always works in our best interests, regardless of how things may appear. This knowledge is more precious than gold!

When we go through trials, it is easy to question God's motives or to charge Him with wrong. If we grumble, "I don't understand why God did [or allowed] this," we are calling His character into question. In so doing we turn ourselves into God's judges. Thus we exalt ourselves above God.

God said to Job, "Shall a faultfinder contend with the Almighty? . . . Will you even put me in the wrong? Will you condemn me that you may be justified?" (Job 40:2, 8).

If we charge God with injustice or unkindness, we are being both unbelievably arrogant and completely inaccurate. "The LORD is just in all his ways, and kind in all his doings" (Psalm 145:17). When people stand before God, their accusations against Him will die in their throats because they will see the truth. Isaiah 45:24 says, "To [the LORD] shall come and be ashamed, all who were incensed against him." They will discover that God is not guilty of any of their charges or accusations. Those "incensed against Him" will behold a God of infinite justice, kindness and holiness, and will hang their heads in shame.

We Exalt Ourselves
When We Take God's Word Lightly

"Christians today," writes Martha Thatcher in *The Freedom of Obedience,* "are information-rich and application-poor. From Sunday schools to seminaries we discuss spiritual information."[2] Often our goal seems to be to transmit knowledge rather than to see people changed. But Christ never said, "If you know these things, you are blessed." He said, "If you know these things, blessed are you *if you do them*" (John 13:17, italics added).

Paul warned both Titus and Timothy about wasting time in vain spiritual discussions that do not produce change in people's lives. Paul sought to further the "knowledge of the truth *which accords with godliness*" (Titus 1:1, italics added). He promoted "divine training that is in faith" (1 Timothy 1:4).

Reading the Bible can become boring if we read it like spectators, instead of realizing we are responsible to obey it. Jesus says, "Why do you call me 'Lord, Lord,' and do not do what I tell you?" (Luke 6:46). The phrase *No, Lord* is a contradiction in terms. If we say "no" to the Lord, then He is not our Lord.

Rather, God reveals Himself to those who humble themselves before Him, who approach the Bible to receive instruction as to how to live their lives. He is God and we are not. The Lord says, "This is the one I esteem: he who is humble and contrite in spirit, and trembles at my word" (Isaiah 66:2, NIV).

THE FEAR OF THE LORD IS A FOUNTAIN OF LIFE

11

When I was a baby Christian, my fear of God was the wrong kind. I was afraid of God's will. *Maybe God wants me to be single forever,* I thought. *Worse yet, maybe He wants me to be a missionary!* As a result of my fears, my heart was not very cooperative. Subconsciously I thought that if I just held onto the reins of my life, perhaps I could prevent God from wrecking it.

I did not realize how insulting these fears were. Like the young woman in the last chapter who considered God "cruel," my thoughts actually demeaned my Creator.

After many years of getting to know God better, I realize now that my thoughts were not only insulting; they were downright ignorant. Today I stand in awe of how kind God has been to me through the years.

Any sin, whether of thought, word or deed, attacks God's character. It dishonors Him because it indicates that we do not believe His way is best. We question His wisdom or His kindness or both. When we sin, we are saying to God, "I don't trust You. I trust me. I want what's best for me; I'm not so sure about You. I'm going with my own plan." Thus we exalt ourselves and demean God at the same time—a nasty combination.

If we fear God's will, we do not fear God biblically. We do not respect Him in the way we should. The healthy, biblical "fear of the Lord" means more than just respecting God for His mighty power. It means more than simply respecting Him as the One to whom we must give account. We must also respect Him by recognizing that He is perfect in wisdom and in kindness. We must acknowledge Him as a good God whose plans are better than our own. Then we will trust and obey Him—cheerfully. "The LORD takes pleasure in those who fear Him, in those who hope in his steadfast love" (Psalm 147:11).

R. C. Sproul writes:

> That the world has little respect for God is vividly seen by the way the world regards His name. His name is tramped through the dirt of this world. It functions as a curse word, a platform for the obscene. No honor. No reverence. No awe before Him.
>
> [In the Lord's prayer] we often confuse the words "Hallowed be thy name" with part of the address as if the words were "hallowed *is* your name." In that case the words would merely be an ascription of praise to God. But that is not how Jesus said it. He uttered it as a petition, as the first petition. We should be praying that God's name be hallowed, that God be regarded as holy.
>
> There is a kind of sequence within the prayer. God's kingdom will never come where His name is not hallowed. His will is not done on earth as it is in heaven if His name is desecrated here. . . . Heaven is a place where reverence for God is total. It is foolish to look for the kingdom anywhere God is not revered.[1]

Everything good starts with respect for God. Satan constantly calls God's character into question, knowing that all sin begins with the suspicion that God is not good. The devil's strategy has not changed since he approached Eve in the Garden. Once he established this suspicion in her mind, disobedience soon followed. Disobedience follows disrespect.

The lies Satan formulates to demean God's character are designed to turn our hearts away from God. Obviously, if our view of God is tainted with thoughts of His being uncaring, unconcerned, unjust, cruel, tyrannical or boring, we will not get very excited about following Him. People who do not want to follow God are people who do not know what God is like. The cure is the truth.

When we see God as He is, we can no more help trusting Him than we can help breathing. "When you see Him as He is," writes Joy Dawson, ". . . it becomes a preposterous thought *not* to obey Him!"[2] We are in a battle and our minds are the battlefield. We must be diligent to reject thoughts that slander God's character.

The Wise Man Built . . . the Foolish Man Built . . . But Why?

You are probably familiar with Jesus' words in Matthew 7:24–27:

> "Every one then who hears these words of mine and does them will be like a wise man who built his house upon the rock; and the rain fell, and the floods came, and the winds blew and beat upon that house, but it did not fall, because it had been founded on the rock. And every one who hears these words of mine and does not do them will be like a foolish man who built his house upon the sand; and the rain fell, and the floods came, and the winds blew and beat against that house and it fell; and great was the fall of it."

In this passage we clearly see the *results* of doing or not doing Jesus' words. But let's ponder the *cause*. Why do some people hear and obey? Why do others hear and not obey? What is going on in the heads of both groups? What do they believe about God? What do they believe about themselves?

The foolish man does not obey because he does not respect God or His words. He has a better plan. The "fear of the LORD is the beginning of wisdom" (Proverbs 9:10), but a fool has no fear of the Lord. He has no room for God's wisdom because he is already wise in his own eyes. He has no room for God because he already has a god. In effect he is saying to God, "Don't cramp my style. I'm running things here. I don't need Your advice."

The bottom line: The foolish man is proud, and his pride makes him unteachable. *He has more regard for himself than for the God of the universe.*

It disturbs me to think that this happens in thousands of churches every week. The pastor speaks the Word of God and people leave unchanged, not adjusting their lives to what God says. How much pride do we reveal in ourselves when we hear the Word of God, then go on living as we always have?

The wise man, on the other hand, hears and obeys God's Word because he respects God. He does not obey reluctantly. His heart embraces God's words. Psalm 112:1 says, "Blessed is the man who fears the LORD, who greatly delights in his commandments!"

With the exception of the Bathsheba/Uriah episode, David is a good example of one who embraced God's words. He made adjustments in his life. "When I think of thy ways," David wrote, "I turn my feet to thy testimonies" (Psalm 119:59).

When our hearts are in this condition, God can do magnificent things in our lives. He can pour out what is in His heart—blessings beyond our imagination. Psalm 31:19 says, "O how abundant is thy goodness, which thou hast laid up for those who fear thee. . . !" In His joy the Lord says in Deuteronomy 5:29: "Oh that they had such a mind as this always, to fear me and to keep all my commandments, that it might go well with them and with their children for ever!" Those who fear God experience the reality of Proverbs 14:27: "The fear of the LORD is a fountain of life."

Look at David's attitude toward God's words in the verses that follow:

> The fear of the LORD is clean, enduring for ever; the ordinances of the LORD are true, and righteous altogether. More to be desired are they than gold, even much fine gold; sweeter also than honey and drippings of the honeycomb. Moreover by them is thy servant warned; in keeping them there is great reward.
>
> Psalm 19:9–11

> Thy testimonies are my delight, they are my counselors.
>
> Psalm 119:24

> The law of thy mouth is better to me than thousands of gold and silver pieces.
>
> verse 72

> I rejoice at thy word like one who finds great spoil.
>
> verse 162

> My soul keeps thy testimonies; I love them exceedingly.
>
> verse 167

A Highway to Holiness

If you want your life to be fully pleasing to God, the fear of the Lord can help you get where you want to go. Paul writes, "Having these promises, beloved, let us cleanse ourselves from all filthiness of the flesh and spirit, *perfecting holiness in the fear of God"* (2 Corinthians 7:1, NKJV, italics added). Unholiness comes from running our own lives—in rebellion against a God we do not respect. Proverbs 16:6 says, "By the fear of the LORD a man avoids evil." The fear of the Lord protects us from going astray. Jeremiah 32:40 says, "I will put the fear of me in their hearts, that they may not turn from me."

As long as we trust Him, we will not rebel against Him. Disobedience indicates that we believe God is less than who He really is. Proverbs 3:5–7 (NIV) gets to the core of the issue:

> Trust in the LORD with all your heart and lean not on your own understanding; in all your ways acknowledge him, and he will make your paths straight. Do not be wise in your own eyes; fear the LORD and shun evil.

We are continually to acknowledge the truth about what God is like. 1 Samuel 12:24 says, "Only fear the Lord, and serve him faithfully with all your heart; *for consider what great things he has done for you*" (italics added).

God often told the Hebrews to set up a memorial so they would not forget some kind and mighty act He had done on their behalf. For example, He directed that stones be set up to remind them that He had dried up the Jordan River for them to walk through, "so that all the peoples of the earth may know that the hand of the LORD is mighty; that you may fear the LORD your God for ever" (Joshua 4:24).

God was also concerned that His people teach their children to fear God. The Lord said to Moses:

> "Gather the people to me, that I may let them hear my words, so that they may learn to fear me all the days that they live upon the earth, and that they may teach their children so."
> Deuteronomy 4:10

First we must model the fear of the Lord by respecting, trusting and obeying God with a cheerful attitude. (We cannot give away what we do not have.) Second, we must treat our children with love, respect and firmness. If they learn to fear God, realizing that His ways are best, they will be O.K.—

in fact, much better than O.K. If they do not fear God, I fear for their future!

Heart Surgery You Can Do Yourself

When we do not respect God, we harden our hearts against Him. Proverbs 28:14 says, "Blessed is the man who fears the LORD always; but he who hardens his heart will fall into calamity." A hard heart and respect for God cannot both fit inside the same person.

In John Bunyan's book *The Holy War,* Diabolos urges the people to resist God, and he tells them how to do it. Above all, he recommends putting on a certain breastplate. "This is a breastplate of iron," he says. "It's a hard heart! Keep it on and mercy won't win you, and judgment won't scare you."[3]

When I go off God's path and need to repent, I often use truth to cure my hardness of heart. Let me use unforgiveness as an example. When someone offends me, I make myself admit two things. First, that God is good and all His ways are good, including His command to forgive. Second, that He is the boss, not me. I repeat these truths several times, until they get down into my heart.

When I acknowledge God in this way, He straightens me out. Or, to put it in biblical terms, He "makes my paths straight."

When I repent, I must turn not only from wrong behaviors, but also from the false beliefs about God that have caused these wrong behaviors. Proverbs 16:6 says, "By the fear of the LORD a man avoids evil." Respect for God is the key.

God provides a good summary of what will happen when His judgments are unveiled: "Those who honor me I will honor, and those who despise me shall be lightly esteemed" (1 Samuel 2:30).

12 PLEASING GOD IN YOUR WORK

Ed made only $4.25 an hour and was not too happy about it. When the foreman asked him to dig the mud out of a form for a driveway, Ed dug without enthusiasm. Later, when the foreman observed Ed's halfhearted efforts, he said, "I'm going to need you to push that shovel a little faster."

"For $4.25 an hour," Ed replied, "this is as fast as I push."

"Then come to the office," the foreman said. "We'll get you your final paycheck."

Proverbs 18:9 declares, "He who is slack in his work is a brother to him who destroys." If we do not obey God's command to work with all our hearts, perhaps our motivation has been stolen. Motivation is stolen not by adverse circumstances but by wrong thinking about those circumstances.

Wrong Thoughts, the Thieves of Motivation

1. *"I don't receive enough salary.* I don't get paid what I deserve, so I guess I work down to the level of my com-

pensation. I don't mean to complain, but my company gets what it pays for."

2. *"I don't receive the recognition I deserve from my superiors.* It's hard not to feel bitter. It's discouraging to give it all I've got and never get a pat on the back or a word of thanks, much less a bonus or promotion. I don't want to work halfheartedly, but when even my best work is not appreciated, what's the use?"

3. *"My work is secular.* If I were involved in ministry, I'd be motivated, but it's hard to get excited about work with no eternal value."

4. *"My boss is a %!&@#.* If I work hard, it'll make my boss look good, and frankly, I don't want my boss to look good. I've talked to my co-workers, and believe me, I'm not the only one who feels this way."

God's solution, revealed in the following passage, destroys these thieves of motivation and transforms our work lives. His solution makes us more alive and brings joy to our daily tasks.

> Slaves, obey in everything those who are your earthly masters, not with eyeservice, as men-pleasers, but in singleness of heart, fearing the Lord. Whatever your task, work heartily, as serving the Lord and not men, knowing that from the Lord you will receive the inheritance as your reward; you are serving the Lord Christ.
>
> Colossians 3:22–24

This passage is not an isolated admonition that applies only to slaves; it is what godliness looks like on the job.

Other Scriptures give similar instructions. When King Jehoshaphat appointed judges, he charged them with these words: "Thus you shall do in the fear of the LORD, in faithfulness, and with your whole heart" (2 Chronicles 19:9). Likewise the Bible tells us that King Hezekiah

> did what was good and right and faithful before the LORD his God. And every work that he undertook in the service of the

house of God and in accordance with the law and the commandments, seeking his God, he did with all his heart, and prospered.

2 Chronicles 31:20–21

It would be hard to imagine circumstances much more adverse than those faced by the slaves Paul was writing to, yet Paul instructed them to please God by working with all their hearts. Those who think they cannot be motivated unless they are paid more should consider that these slaves did not get paid at all.

Those demotivated by the thought that their work is secular should take note that Paul was writing not to ministers but to slaves. No work is secular if it is done for the glory of God! We can please God and earn eternal reward, whatever the task!

And finally, to those demotivated by dislike for their boss or by insufficient recognition, Paul wrote, in effect, "You're working for the wrong boss! Don't work as unto men. Work as a God-pleaser. It is from the Lord that you will receive your reward."

Menpleasers work harder when their bosses are around. They lack integrity in their work. They will also lack eternal reward from their work. "Do the thing that is right even when the boss isn't looking," writes Alfred Haake, "because the boss isn't a criterion. The real boss is standing alongside you every moment of your life."[1]

Ephesians 6:5 says to work *"with fear and trembling . . . as to Christ"* (italics added). If we simply see the truth about our awesome opportunity each day in our work—to serve the living God Himself—it would indeed cause us to tremble! Paul is assuming we would have sense enough to tremble if Christ Himself were to give us a task. Now he is asking us to tremble if Christ gives us a task indirectly, through an earthly master. You are serving the Lord Christ! What an honor!

123

God's Standards for Our Work

Most people have certain standards for their work. Some do an excellent job in whatever they put their hand to. Some do a good job. Some do an adequate job. Some do just enough to get by. Likewise, some students are "A" students. Some are "B" students. Some are "C" students. And some students are not students!

But God's standards are different. His ways are not our ways. According to Colossians 3:23, God is interested primarily in the answers to two questions: Did you put your heart into it? Did you do it for Me?

In his book *The Fight*, John White describes the transformation of his work life in college:

> I remember the relief I felt when I quit worrying about exams. I was studying human pathology at the time. . . . With half my mind I was reading and with the other half I was worrying about such questions as: Am I really absorbing this stuff? Is it likely to come up in an exam? Am I going too slowly? . . . Why is this so boring?
>
> From somewhere the thought came: Why not read this chapter *as unto the Lord?*
>
> Not worry about exams? I caught my breath. One part of me knew that I would experience relief and enjoy my work more. Another part of me rebelled. The suggestion seemed dangerous. My examiners were not interested in godly conscientiousness but in my covering the material.
>
> The struggle was brief and I opted for godliness. I was sick of the drudgery of studying for grades. . . . "For you, Lord," became my motivation.
>
> To my joy I found his yoke easy and his burden light so that I studied with rest in my soul. Pathology grew more interesting. . . . The drudgery melted away and a sense of satisfaction and gratitude took its place. Exams or no exams, I would study for God. And I took time off to play tennis with a carefree spirit.

[Now] I was responsible to use my study time in a way that pleased God. I . . . enjoyed what I was doing. I certainly learned a lot more, though how this affected my marks I do not know. Nor do I care. I was no longer working for grades but for Christ. Study had become for me [a calling]. . . . Of course I would slip back from time to time [to my old attitudes]. Pleasing Christ in my studies was like learning a new swimming stroke. It had to be practiced. Yet my studies were never the same again.[2]

The Blessings of Obedience

What happens when we take God's instructions seriously in our work lives? Our work turns into an act of love toward God. Because we are so in love with Him, we work with "singleness of heart, as to Christ" (Ephesians 6:5). We work with purity of motive and purity of devotion.

Our perspective changes. Our labor ceases to be laborious. Whether we work at home or away from it, we begin to see our labor as a privilege. Instead of seeing responsibilities, we see opportunities.

Widespread obedience among Christians would change not only us as individuals; it would change our society. If we worked as unto the Lord with all of our hearts, we would begin to rise within our professions. How do you as an employer feel about an employee who works diligently even when nobody is watching? Who is eager to help? Who serves joyfully? Who is content? Who is honest? It is not hard to imagine someone with these attitudes being promoted. If godliness on the job causes us to rise to positions of greater influence, we can use our influence to bless more people and to advance God's Kingdom.

Let's pay heed, then, to the counsel God gave Asa: "'But you, take courage! Do not let your hands be weak, for your work shall be rewarded.' When Asa heard these words . . . he took courage" (2 Chronicles 15:7–8).

13 SEIZING THE TIME

One of the ways we prepare ourselves for the Judgment Seat of Christ is by making every day count for the Kingdom of God. Ephesians 5:15–17 says:

> Look carefully then how you walk, not as unwise men but as wise, making the most of the time, because the days are evil. Therefore do not be foolish, but understand what the will of the Lord is.

We are always in danger of becoming preoccupied with things that do not matter, with things that are not eternal, with things that are not the will of God. To make the most of our time, we have to bring it under control, to "seize the time." Since God commands us to do it, we can do so—even if, up until now, we have been disorganized. What God commands us to do, He enables us to do.

Seizing our time involves getting better control of our lives and making the most of our opportunities. The benefits of seizing our time are enormous. Our lives become more effective, more enjoyable and less stressful. Most important, our lives become more honoring to God.

Start with Vision

Good time management begins with vision. Take stock of the gifts and talents God has given you. Consider any calling you believe He has put on your life, regardless of your age. Is there a particular person or group God has called you to bless? Tell Him you want to be effective for His Kingdom, that you want to do His will. What do you think God is calling you to accomplish? Now take some time to brainstorm and dream. As you do this, you will begin to see future possibilities. Write down your ideas. Don't worry if they sound unrealistic. If God is calling you to do something, He is sufficient to accomplish it through you.

Getting a clear vision in your thoughts of what God wants you to do will help you act it out in reality. If you want to accomplish something significant, you must first *see* something significant. Significant vision precedes significant success. Vision without action is merely a dream. Action without vision just passes the time. Vision with action can change the world.

The next step, however, is not to get busy, but to prepare. God has to shape and prepare us as a potter prepares a vessel. We must become what God wants us to become before we can do what God wants us to do.

Even if we clearly understand God's vision for our lives, it is dangerous to run ahead of Him. Moses understood the vision—that God wanted to deliver the Hebrews out of Egyptian slavery—but Moses took action forty years before he was properly prepared (see Acts 7:23–25, 30). Likewise, Abraham and Sarah understood the vision—that Abraham would become the father of many nations—but they did not wait for God's timing. Sarah brought Hagar into the picture, and the Middle East has suffered turmoil among the descendants of Ishmael and Isaac ever since.

God will not expand our influence for His Kingdom until we first learn to be faithful over little. We need to bloom where we are planted. What tasks has God already given you to do? Do them well. And, most importantly, make sure your personal relationship with Him is growing and deepening. Peter Lord says, "You take care of the depth of your life, and God will take care of the breadth of your ministry."

How can we make every day count for the Kingdom? Let's discuss the nuts and bolts of good time management.

The Distinction between Purposes and Goals

A man took some time to dream and to formulate a vision for the upcoming year. On a piece of paper he wrote, "I want to be a better husband. I want to be a better father. I want to grow spiritually." This might look like a great list of goals, but actually these are not goals at all. They are purposes or good intentions. Unfortunately our good intentions do not always affect our daily lives. That is where goals come in.

Purposes are general statements regarding the direction in which we would like to move. *Goals*, on the other hand, are specific statements regarding measurable accomplishments. In *Living in Light of Eternity* Stacy and Paula Rinehart write:

> Once you have articulated [a] life purpose, the next step of establishing goals follows naturally. *Goals* are . . . measurable objectives that reflect your larger life purposes. They enable you to reject the superfluous, and then to concentrate on the direction in which God is leading you. They make it possible for a life purpose to hop off the paper and into your life.[1]

Let's return to the man who wants to be a better husband and father. What action-oriented goals can he set? He needs to move out of vagueness into the realm of the well-defined.

The more specific he is, the more direction he will have. "Better husband" goals, for example, might be:

- Attend a marriage enrichment retreat with my wife by the end of the year.
- Read *The Marriage Builder* by Larry Crabb within the next two months.
- Schedule a weekend vacation without the children.

"Better father" goals might include:

- Take each of my children out for a special date by the end of this month.
- Read *What Kids Need Most in a Dad* by Tim Hansel within three months.
- Plan and schedule a fishing trip with my son.

Well-set goals add enthusiasm to life. Once you have a goal, life is different. If you cannot get excited about where you are, at least you can be excited about where you are going!

For about three years I had a good intention I never acted on. Even though I want my kids to be able to go to college, I had not saved a penny for their education. Several times during those years, I kicked myself over this but never did anything about it. Good intentions do not have the power to move us to constructive action as goals do. When I finally attached a goal to my good intention, things started to happen.

I made it my goal to make an appointment with a financial planner. As soon as I adopted that goal, I felt completely different. I still had not saved a penny, but the burden was gone. The financial planner helped me set up a direct deposit from my paycheck into an account dedicated as a college fund. The amount was small, but it was a start.

A goal takes our focus off the present circumstances and puts it on future possibilities. A well-set goal moves us to action.

Six Characteristics of Well-Set Goals

1. WELL-SET GOALS ARE WRITTEN

You might be a person who does not write your goals down, yet you are still effective. But perhaps you can be even more effective if you commit your goals to writing. Here are some of the advantages:

A. Writing your goals brings them into sharper focus. Writing your goals helps to crystallize your thinking. In Habakkuk 2:2 God says, "Write the vision and make it plain on tablets, that he may *run* who reads it" (NKJV, italics added). Written goals are like lane markers on a track; they tell us where to run. After we have a written plan, we are ready to run. We have taken the time to ponder where we want to invest our lives and are then ready to propel ourselves in the right direction. Without lane markers, we are more likely to waste time by hesitating or by running in the wrong direction.

"We can know whether what we are doing is absurd only after we have identified the goals we are trying to achieve," says Charles Hughes. "Until this has been done, there can be no assurance that effort expended will be in the right direction."[2]

B. If your goals are written, you are less inclined to forget them. Someone once said, "Weak ink is better than a strong memory."

If you are driving to a city you have never been to before, you need a map. The same is true if you are living through a day you have never lived through before. Life can get so crazy that it is easy to forget what in the world you are trying to accomplish! A list of goals helps you get through your day without getting lost.

Wise travelers keep their maps close by. They look at them when they need to make sure they are on the right road and when they need to know what to do next. A list of goals performs the same functions. Keep the list close by. Don't lose sight of your goals!

Start by setting some long-term goals that emanate from your life purposes. Your daily goals should be steps that help you move toward the achievement of your long-term goals.

C. Writing your goals increases your commitment to them. We tend to be more serious about goals we have committed to writing, which is why writing our goals is commitment step number one. The other commitment step is to assign a deadline to each goal, which we will discuss later.

D. If you write your goals down, you can cross them off. It is very satisfying to determine beforehand what we want to accomplish, and then to mark these items off when done.

2. WELL-SET GOALS ARE REASONABLE AND REACHABLE

Some people build frustration into their lives by adopting goals that are unreasonably high, or by adopting too many goals for a given time period.

3. WELL-SET GOALS ARE MEASURABLE AND SPECIFIC

We should phrase our goals in such a way that we will know exactly *when* each goal has been accomplished. Well-set goals are expressed in terms of results, not activity.

I started writing down my daily goals about fourteen years ago. At the time I was teaching economics. To prepare future lectures, I often included "Read economics" as one of my goals for the day. Unfortunately my goal was neither measurable nor specific. How much did I need to read to attain my goal? The whole book? Certain pages? How much was enough? It was not clear. It would have been more effective to write, "Read chapter 14" or, "Read pages 205–228." When a goal has been expressed in measurable terms, we are likely to proceed more purposefully.

A seminary professor once invited me to do a seminar on goal-setting for one of his classes. I encouraged the class to express what they wanted to accomplish in measurable and specific ways. After the class, as the students were leaving, the professor pulled me aside and said, "I've got a great example for you! When I was working on my dissertation, my daily goal for the first few months was 'Work five hours on dissertation today.' Even when I put in five hours, I got almost nothing done. Then I changed my goal to 'Write five pages today.' It was like night and day. I started zooming! Some days it took me two hours to write five pages; some days it took me twelve, but the difference was, I was results-oriented instead of just logging in time."

We must be careful not to confuse activity with accomplishment. Busyness can be deceptive. We can be busy doing things that keep us from more important things. We can be busy doing things we should not be doing at all. "Goals can take you out of the endless circles of activity," writes Lewis Timberlake, "and point you to the road of accomplishment."[3]

Avoid maintenance goals like "Run three miles every day" or "Spend an hour with the Lord every day." The problem with maintenance goals is that they cannot be accomplished within a finite time period. The way these goals have been phrased, you can never attain them and cross them off. Failure and frustration are almost inevitable. Even if you do them from now until you die, it is too late then to cross them off!

Obviously I am not trying to discourage anyone from getting regular exercise or spending time with the Lord daily. But make your goals attainable within a finite time period. One easy solution is to change your wording and redefine your goal. You might say, for instance, "It's my *practice* to run three miles every day, but my *goal* is to run three miles *today.*"

4. WELL-SET GOALS HAVE A SELF-IMPOSED DEADLINE

Deadlines are powerful. Why does so much get accomplished as a deadline draws near? Deadlines help us overcome procrastination, distractions and indecision. So give yourself a time to shoot for. Long-term goals need a date deadline, whereas daily goals need a time-of-day deadline.

If I have a goal but no deadline, all I have said is that I will accomplish this goal sometime in the future. The future is a long time! Deadlines are the foundation of commitment. If I am talking to my son, there is a big difference between my saying, "Timmy, I'm going to take you camping one day," and, "Timmy, I'm going to take you camping by the end of this month." A deadline changes everything! Now I must make this thing happen.

Deadlines are a painful topic for many of us. Deadlines bring pressure. Why would we want to impose them on ourselves? Fortunately, if we keep certain principles in mind while we set deadlines, they can actually reduce our stress. The first one is just common sense—but it is still a challenge.

A. Be realistic about the time it takes to perform a given task. Murphy's second law states, "Everything takes longer than you think."

B. Add time for unexpected problems and opportunities. I have heard three theories as to why habitually late people are late. Since I fall into this category, these theories interest me.

The first one is not very nice. It says habitually late people are late because they have not chosen to honor the people they are meeting. I admit reluctantly that there might be some truth to this. After all, if our appointment were with the President, we would probably be on time. (On the other hand, sometimes we are late to one appointment because we stayed late helping somebody in our last appointment.)

The second theory is that late people do not try as hard as other people to be on time. I see little merit in this theory. Sometimes I am like a tornado trying to get ready and I am still late.

The third theory, in my opinion, is the most powerful and helpful: Habitually late people are late because they try to be on time. On-time people are on time because they try to be early.

Let's say a habitually late person has a two o'clock meeting. *It takes twenty minutes to get there,* he reasons, *so I need to leave at 1:40. . . . Yipes! I'm on fumes. I need to stop for gas or I'm not going to make it. . . . Late again!*

Because they try to be on time, any unexpected delay makes them late. But they always have a reason: "If I didn't have to stop for gas, I'd have been on time." But most habitually late people never stop to wonder about on-time people. ("Gee, I wonder if their cars use gas, too?")

Unexpected delays happen to everybody, but some people have learned to expect the unexpected and build in a buffer. They train themselves to try to get places a few minutes early. What a good way to meet a deadline—and what a great stress-reducer!

C. Set your personal deadline before the system-imposed deadline. April 15 is the Internal Revenue Service deadline for paying personal income taxes. Why not adopt an earlier date?

I wish I had learned to do this earlier in my life. One year I got to the post office at midnight on April 15. (Actually, I did not get there until 12:05 because I was trying to be on time!) I was not alone. There was a long line of cars there. We were setting blood pressure records.

D. On larger projects, assign a deadline to each step. If someone gave you a three-pound salami, could you swallow it? When I pose this question to my students, many look at me in bewilderment, probably thinking something like, *If I tried to swallow a salami, I'd die.*

A few raise their hands immediately, however, to indicate they *could* swallow it. One such student had a silly grin on his face. I asked him how he would do it and why he was grinning. He replied, "I realized you didn't say I had to do it in one bite, so I thought about cutting up the salami and having it on Ritz crackers. I *love* Ritz crackers."

Do you face a large project that intimidates you? Do you walk around it in awe? Does the intimidation spur you on or does it paralyze you? If you feel overwhelmed, use the salami technique. Divide the large, difficult job into small, manageable, bite-sized pieces. Then assign a deadline to each step.

Were it not for the salami technique, you would not be reading these words because I would never have written them. I despised writing for the first 33 years of my life. My English teachers told me to write a rough draft, but I thought, *Why waste the time?* I saved a few steps and skipped right to the final draft. But every paragraph, like a three-pound salami, almost killed me, because I tried to write, edit and polish all in one step. Now I have learned the secret of flinging my thoughts, disjointed as they may be, into a rough draft and not worrying about how they sound. Later I go back and try to make my writing more forceful, precise and interesting.

The secret? Dividing the task into bite-sized pieces.

If we want to accomplish great things, we do not have to leap over mountains. We have to learn to take one step at a time.

5. WELL-SET GOALS DEPEND ON YOUR OWN BEHAVIOR

Don't base your goals on what you hope others will do. Frustration results from adopting goals outside your control. (Please review chapter 7.)

6. WELL-SET GOALS ARE PRIORITIZED

Alec Mackenzie in his book *The Time Trap* recounts that during the 1920s, Charles Schwab, the president of Bethlehem Steel, called in a management consultant named Ivy Lee and said, "Mr. Lee, if you can show me how to get more done, I will pay you any fee within reason."

I imagine Mr. Lee liked the way the conversation was going. He asked Mr. Schwab to write down everything he hoped to accomplish the next day. Mr. Schwab listed several items. Then Mr. Lee asked, "If you were driving home from work tomorrow, and only one of these things had gotten done, which one would you like it to be?"

Mr. Schwab put a *1* next to that item.

Then Mr. Lee asked, "If you only accomplished two, which would you like the second one to be?"

Mr. Schwab put a *2* next to that one.

And so on.

Finally Mr. Lee said, "When you get to your office tomorrow, begin working on your top-priority item, and stick with it until it has been accomplished. Then start the second item. At the end of the day, if you haven't finished your whole list, that's O.K. At least you've devoted yourself to the things that matter most, without getting distracted by items of lesser consequence. If this works for you, share it with your staff, and then send me a check for whatever you think the idea is worth."

A few months later, Ivy Lee received a check in the mail for $25,000.

During the next two decades Charles Schwab built Bethlehem Steel into the largest independent steel producer in the world. He later testified that the lesson he learned from Ivy Lee was the most helpful one he ever learned during his business career.[4]

I find that adhering (or not adhering) to this principle makes a dramatic difference in my life. Surprisingly, if I complete my top-priority item, I usually go home with a sense of satisfaction, even if I am unable to accomplish anything else. If I start working without first focusing on priorities, on the other hand, I often leave feeling unsatisfied, even if I accomplish a large number of low-priority tasks. I feel more like a hamster running on a wheel.

Sometimes I begin my workday by trying to get some low-priority tasks out of the way. Some of these "small, quick" items do not turn out to be so small and quick. Often one grabs me by the foot and wrestles me to the ground. Cleaning up low-priority items first is a pathway to frustration.

When I was a new Christian, I had my time with the Lord at the end of each day, when other things were out of the way— so I could really focus. I cannot tell you how often my time with the Lord dropped off the end of the day. By the time I got to that last item, either my time was gone or my energy was depleted.

The word *priority* indicates not only what is important, but also what should be tackled *prior* to other things. Your priorities should be reflected in the deadlines you set. Attach your earliest deadline, whenever possible, to your top-priority task.

God wants us to live for those things that matter most. To live worthwhile lives, we have to give ourselves to worthwhile goals. To prepare for the Judgment Seat of Christ, we need to build our lives around goals that will matter for all eternity. We must live this day for *that* day.

Accomplish More by Focusing on Less

When Marcy and I bought our first house, there were two huge peach trees in the yard. One day I noticed that these trees had sprouted hundreds of peach blossoms. Visions of peach cobbler started dancing in my head. In a couple of weeks every blossom was replaced by a marble-sized peach. A few weeks later they were the size of golfballs. A few weeks later they were still the size of golfballs. Then they turned brown.

Despite our high hopes, we did not get a single peach worth eating that year. We watered the trees and sprayed for bugs, but failed to do one vital thing: We did not prune the trees. As a result the nutrients absorbed by the roots were divided among too many branches. Lots of branches. No cobbler.

I relate the story because it provides an interesting picture of our lives. Are we like pruned or unpruned trees? Are we dissipating our attention and energy by dividing it in too many directions? Or are we focusing on a few important things so that we can be fruitful in the things that matter most?

When you were a kid, did you ever use a magnifying glass to try to set a leaf or piece of paper on fire? It's a challenge! Until you focus the sunlight on one tiny spot, nothing much happens. Likewise, if we want to accomplish something great, nothing much happens until we learn to focus completely on the project at hand.

Why do we put things on top of our desks when we are not ready to work on them? Isn't it because we do not want to forget them? We put them in a place where they will grab our attention. The problem is, it works! Every time our eyes wander from the task at hand and we see the other items, our train of thought is broken. By using a good filing system and a daily planner, we can reduce visual distractions and improve our focus.

In Luke 10 we find Martha scurrying about, feeling overloaded and overwhelmed. Finally she complains to Jesus. His answer may have surprised her: "Martha, Martha, you are anxious and troubled about many things; few things are needful, or only one" (verses 41–42, alternate marginal translation). Martha obviously thought many things were needful and thus felt overwhelmed.

Observes Charlie Shedd:

> Our heavenly Father never gives us too much to do. Men will. We assign ourselves an overload, but never the Lord. He knows what He wants from each of us, and there is plenty of time in His day for things essential to His plan. We do Him a grave injustice when we fall into the habit of compulsive overwork. We sin when we pressure out His wishes for assignments that have not been filtered through divine judgment.[5]

And Elisabeth Elliot offers solid advice:

> I wrote to a friend, telling her the things on my roster for which I needed her prayers. It was a long list, more than I felt I could possibly accomplish.

"'Thy list be done' is what I'm praying for you these days," she wrote back. It is a good prayer for a disciple to pray. I am all for making lists of what needs to be done (and I am exhilarated by checking them off when finished!). But the lists must be reviewed daily with the Lord, asking Him to delete whatever is not on His list for us, so that before we go to bed it will be possible to say, "I have finished the work You gave me to do."[6]

As we review our lists with our Lord, setting godly goals and making every day count for the Kingdom of God, we prepare ourselves for the Judgment Seat of Christ.

14 CROWNS OF GOD'S PLEASURE

an the God who spoke the universe into existence do a good job rewarding those who please Him? God's rewards are more wonderful than any human mind has ever been able to imagine: "Eye hath not seen, nor ear heard, neither have entered into the heart of man, the things which God hath prepared for them that love him" (1 Corinthians 2:9, KJV).

The Bible speaks of crowns that will be won by those with whom God is pleased. They are expressions of His delight.

1. The crown of life: for faithfulness in trial
2. The crown of righteousness: for loving His appearing
3. The crown of glory: for shepherding
4. The crown of rejoicing: for soulwinning

God's crowns are not just for those in full-time ministry. All of us, laypersons and clergy alike, are told to run in such a way that we will win the prize.

1. The Crown of Life

The crown of life rewards the believer's faithfulness during trials. The Lord will reward those who accept trials with joy:

> Count it all joy, my brethren, when you meet various trials, for you know that the testing of your faith produces steadfastness. . . . Blessed is the man who endures trial, for when he has stood the test he will receive the crown of life which God has promised to those who love him.
>
> James 1:2–3, 12

These verses reveal that enduring testing and loving God are connected. Those who really love God are those mindful of His love for them. Being aware of God's love causes us to trust Him, even in adversity. We are thus able to meet trials with joy and hope. Regardless of how bad things may appear, God wants us to trust in His kindness and in the fact that "in all things God works for the good of those who love him, who have been called according to his purpose" (Romans 8:28, NIV).

Likewise God wanted the Hebrews to trust Him in the wilderness when facing adversity. God had rescued them from Egyptian slavery with mighty demonstrations of His power and kindness. Three days after God parted the Red Sea, the children of Israel found themselves with no water. God was testing them. Would they trust Him? No, they began to complain and rebel.

God gave them a total of ten tests and ten times they flunked. They were faithless in trial. Their problem: spiritual forgetfulness.

> They forgot what he had done, and the miracles that he had shown them. . . .They did not keep in mind his power, or the day when he redeemed them from the foe.
>
> Psalm 78:11, 42

In response to one of their trials, the Hebrews said, "Because the LORD hated us he has brought us forth out of the land of Egypt, to give us into the hand of the Amorites, to destroy us" (Deuteronomy 1:27). They came to ridiculous and rebellious conclusions because they did not remember prior manifestations of His kindness.

141

If we respond to trials with self-pity and complaining, we are probably making the same mistake.

Many years ago I wrote this in my journal: "God wants you to thank Him for His blessings by name every day." For a number of years I did nothing; then I rediscovered what I had written. Since then giving thanks to God has become one of the biggest blessings of my life. Sometimes when I begin my quiet time, my heart seems as cold as ice. But by the time I acknowledge that the God of the universe cares for me personally, that He has good plans for my life, that He has already delivered me from numerous forms of bondage, that He continues to work in my heart, and that He even uses me to bless others, I feel like climbing onto the roof and shouting, "Praise God!"

We are drowning in God's blessings—if we would but acknowledge them. When we are ungrateful, it is not because we lack blessings. All that is necessary for us to stop being thankful for a blessing, no matter how wonderful it is, is to enjoy it for a long time without interruption. Unfortunately we become so accustomed to our blessings (including our health, work and loved ones) that we do not acknowledge their significance. They are manifestations of the Father's love toward us.

A God of such magnificent love is worthy of our total trust. Imagine the special honor and dignity when those who continue to love the Lord in the midst of trial hear the words, "Please step forward. Receive the crown of life!"

2. The Crown of Righteousness

Paul mentions a second crown in a letter written on the eve of his own death:

> I have fought the good fight, I have finished the race, I have kept the faith. Henceforth there is laid up for me the crown of righteousness, which the Lord, the righteous judge, will award to me on that Day, and not only to me but also to all who have loved his appearing.
>
> 2 Timothy 4:7–8

Although Paul was awaiting his trial in Rome, he was less concerned about appearing before the high court of Rome than he was about standing before the Judgment Seat of Christ. He declared that a special crown of righteousness awaits the lovers of the Lord's appearing.

What causes someone to love the Lord's appearing? Jesus provides the answer in His parable about servants of a master who goes away on a journey (see Matthew 24:44–51). The servants who love their master's appearing are those who love their master and obey his instructions during his absence. Jesus says,

> "He who has my commandments and keeps them, he it is who loves me; and he who loves me will be loved by my Father, and I will love him and manifest myself to him."
>
> John 14:21

As Christ manifests Himself in increasing measure, Christians who practice obedience enjoy a walk with the Lord that is very intimate. They cannot wait to see Him face to face!

3. The Crown of Glory

A third crown, the crown of glory, awaits those who out of right motives shepherd God's people:

> Shepherd the flock of God which is among you, serving as overseers, not by compulsion but willingly, not for dishonest gain but eagerly; nor as being lords over those entrusted to you, but being examples to the flock; and when the Chief Shepherd appears, you will receive the crown of glory that does not fade away.
>
> 1 Peter 5:2–4, NKJV

Shepherds are not merely to tell the sheep how to live; they are to demonstrate how to live. God will reward those who serve eagerly, who see their labor as a privilege.

In Ezekiel 34:2–4 God speaks against selfish, authoritarian shepherds:

> "Ho, shepherds of Israel who have been feeding yourselves! Should not shepherds feed the sheep? You eat the fat, you clothe yourselves with the wool, you slaughter the fatlings; but you do not feed the sheep. The weak you have not strengthened, the sick you have not healed, the crippled you have not bound up, the strayed you have not brought back, the lost you have not sought, and with force and harshness you have ruled them."

This passage expresses God's heart of kindness toward His sheep as well as His job description for His shepherds. How well Jesus fulfilled that job description! He provides not only the example but also the strength to follow His example.

The crown of glory is reserved for those who have the same heart Jesus has toward His sheep, described in John 10:11: "I am the good shepherd. The good shepherd lays down his life for the sheep."

4. The Crown of Rejoicing

The crown of rejoicing is the soulwinner's crown. The apostle Paul writes:

> What is our hope, our joy, or the crown in which we will glory in the presence of our Lord Jesus when he comes? Is it not you? Indeed, you are our glory and joy.
>
> 1 Thessalonians 2:19–20, NIV

> Therefore, my brethren, whom I love and long for, my joy and my crown, stand firm thus in the Lord, my beloved.
>
> Philippians 4:1

It is not hard to understand God's eagerness to reward those who bring the lost to Him. Imagine being the parent of a lost

144

child who has been missing for several days. After diligent searching, a friend finds your son or daughter and brings your child home. How would you feel toward that friend? You would be grateful to that person for the rest of your life!

But we are not always geared toward evangelism. Brent Wallace, who assisted Rick and me in the writing of this book, once shared this incident from his boyhood:

> When I was nine years old I went fishing with a friend at a lake near his house. As we fished, an older man walked by. On seeing us, he stopped and said in a disgusted voice, "There are no fish in this lake!" We reeled in our lines, packed up our tackle boxes and went home.

Brent's story reminds me of my former approach to evangelism and why I was no good at it. I was hindered by negative thinking; Satan had me beaten before I even got my line into the water. I assumed people would not be receptive. I was as effective as a salesman convinced that nobody wants the product.

Lately, however, God has been impressing me with certain convictions:

1. A relationship with Him is *exactly* what unbelievers are searching for, whether they realize it or not. God put a void within all of us that only He can fill. Therefore, it is not just unlikely that unbelievers will find fulfillment elsewhere; it is impossible.

2. When sharing the Gospel with a group, I used to hope that one or two would respond. Now, realizing that *everyone* is yearning to fill the void within, I am learning to go after the whole crowd, as Paul and Peter did: "'Repent, and be baptized *every one of you* in the name of Jesus Christ for the forgiveness of your sins.' . . . There were added that day about three thousand souls" (Acts 2:38, 41, italics added); and: "The times of igno-

rance God overlooked, but now he commands *all men everywhere* to repent" (Acts 17:30, italics added).

Even Jeremiah, who saw little response from the people, was instructed by God to go after the whole crowd: "Do not hold back a word. It may be they will listen, and *every one* turn from his evil way" (Jeremiah 26:2–3, italics added).

This new perspective did not come overnight. I still have to meditate on these truths to keep out the initiative-stealing lies.

Because nothing is impossible with God, we must guard against thinking that anyone is beyond redemption. The woman at the well had had five husbands and was living with a man who was not her husband. She may have appeared an unlikely candidate for receiving the Gospel, but Jesus knew she was thirsty for living water. And after this incident Jesus said to His disciples:

> "I tell you, lift up your eyes, and see how the fields are already white for harvest. He who reaps receives wages, and gathers fruit for eternal life, so that sower and reaper may rejoice together."
>
> John 4:35–36

Recently I have been thinking a lot about a particular Scripture: "He who sows sparingly will also reap sparingly, and he who sows bountifully will also reap bountifully" (2 Corinthians 9:6). Reaping refers to both souls and reward. Do we Christians approach sowing as seriously as a farmer does? If a farmer approached sowing as I have approached evangelistic sowing during most of my Christian life, he and his family would starve to death! What farmer could make a living if he planted a couple of seeds every few months? It is better than planting nothing, but there would not be much of a harvest. If we saw what was at stake, we would be more motivated than any farmer on the planet!

If we wait for the perfect opportunity to share the Gospel (or a tract) with someone, we may find it never comes. Ecclesiastes 11:4 warns us, "He who observes the wind will not sow; and he who regards the clouds will not reap."

Sometimes I feel neither inspired nor motivated to do evangelism. Recently, however, I had this thought: *What kind of farmer would I be if each day I checked out my feelings to see if I felt like sowing that day?* A good farmer focuses not on his feelings, but on the harvest he wants, and he does his job. Psalm 126:6 says, "He that goes forth weeping, bearing the seed for sowing, shall come home with shouts of joy, bringing his sheaves with him."

Satan does all he can to persuade us not to sow. He attempts to discourage us, to convince us that our labor is in vain. Why even try? If a farmer thought his labor was in vain, he would stop working. A farmer continues to labor, even under difficult conditions, because of one thing: He believes in the power of seeds. He is motivated by the hope in his heart.

The Word of God says to us, "Be steadfast, immovable, always abounding in the work of the Lord, knowing that in the Lord your labor is not in vain" (1 Corinthians 15:58). And: "In the morning sow your seed, and at evening withhold not your hand; for you do not know which will prosper, this or that, or whether both alike will be good" (Ecclesiastes 11:6). And finally: "Let us not grow weary in well-doing, for in due season we shall reap, if we do not lose heart" (Galatians 6:9).

God Wants Our Reward to Be Great

God reveals what is at stake at the Judgment Seat—not because He does not like us, but because He loves us! He wants to place crowns upon our heads and has graciously provided us with opportunity to prepare.

15

OLYMPIC MOTIVATION

I magine a teacher announcing that all his students will receive the same grade, regardless of whether they show up for class, hand in their homework or do well on exams. If this teacher severs the connection between performance and reward, what do you think the outcome will be?

Or imagine that everyone trying out for the next Olympic games will make the team simply by showing up. It does not matter whether a candidate is in shape or not. He might be a high jumper who weighs four hundred pounds, but as long as he can roll over the bar, he is in. Furthermore, an announcement proclaims that all distinctions in prizes have been eliminated. Rather than a gold medal, silver medal, bronze medal or no medal, everyone will get the same prize, regardless of performance. What do you think the results would be? How motivated do you think athletes would be in their training?

One last scenario. What if the truths about the Judgment Seat and eternal reward were somehow removed from the Church? The relevant Scriptures would not have to be cut out of every Bible. But if no one preached or taught or discussed these matters, what would the Church be like?

Most of the Church would be as it is today—much like the students in the first scenario, much like the athletes in the second.

If we never think about reward, or if we hold the false notion that all will receive the same reward in heaven, we will lack motivation God intended us to have.

How many Christians do you know who seek to please God with as much diligence and intensity as an Olympic athlete seeking a gold medal? What would happen to the Church if Christians came to believe that the rewards God wants to give us exceed the value of an Olympic gold medal by a millionfold? That is not an overexaggeration; it is an underexaggeration.

The one thing that will provide us with the motivation we need is the truth. If we realize what is actually at stake, we will be more motivated than the most motivated Olympic champion!

Paul expresses his yearning that we understand this truth in the following passage:

> Do you not know that in a race all the runners run, but only one gets the prize? Run in such a way as to get the prize. Everyone who competes in the games goes into strict training. They do it to get a crown that will not last; but we do it to get a crown that will last forever.
>
> 1 Corinthians 9:24–25, NIV

Paul likely had the Isthmian games in mind when he wrote this passage. The Isthmian games of the Greek peninsula were a forerunner of our modern Olympic games. The umpire of the games presided from a raised platform called the judgment seat. From there he watched the events and ultimately rewarded the winners.

When the New Testament speaks of winning a reward, it often takes the form of a crown. The crown mentioned in this passage from 1 Corinthians 9 is the victor's crown—the symbol of honor and achievement. The victors in the Isthmian games were exempted from taxation for the rest of their lives, and their children could attend school without paying tuition. Not bad. But it pales in comparison to what God wants to bestow.

If those athletes were willing to go into strict training to earn a perishable crown, what should we be willing to do to win an imperishable crown—a crown of surpassing worth that will last forever?

> Train yourself in godliness; for while bodily training is of some value, godliness is of value in every way, as it holds promise for the present life and also for the life to come.
>
> 1 Timothy 4:7–8

The following Scripture reflects the welcome Olympic champions receive when they return to their hometowns:

> For if you do these things, you will never fall, and you will receive a *rich welcome* into the eternal kingdom of our Lord and Savior Jesus Christ.
>
> 2 Peter 1:10–11, NIV, italics added

Although each Olympic gold medal winner receives a bucketful of glory, the bucket has a hole in the bottom. The glory seeps out, fading away with each passing year. The glory of God's rewards, on the other hand, never fades! God calls us to train and run in such a way that we will win a crown of unfading glory.

Running to Win

The mature believer is aware of an intense challenge: He must adopt a pattern of responsible discipline to fulfill God's purpose for his life. Paul writes:

> I do not run like a man running aimlessly; I do not fight like a man beating the air. No, I beat my body and make it my slave

so that after I have preached to others, I myself will not be disqualified for the prize.

1 Corinthians 9:26–27, NIV

Paul does not run without a goal in mind. He does not shadow-box or fail to make his punches count. He uses two verbs concerning his treatment of his own body, which imply the utmost in rigorous control.

When Paul says, "I beat my body," he uses a strong word meaning "to strike under the eye" or "to beat black and blue." His body, Paul says, must never become the enemy of his spiritual purpose, so he buffets it! He also says he makes his body his slave. Understand this intensity! Paul is determined that his body might serve and not hinder his progress in pleasing his God.

When athletes train to be Olympic champions, intense discipline is a means to that end. They are not masochists, nor are they engaging in self-abasement or self-flagellation. Rather, they seek a prize and consider their sacrifice small compared to the value of that prize. When they wake up early in the morning to train, they do not let their bodies control them. They do not ask their bodies, "Do you feel like getting up at 4:30 or would you rather sleep late? Do you feel like eating a healthy breakfast or would you prefer a doughnut?" Likewise, we must make our bodies subject to us so that we can run in such a way as to win the prize.

When Paul talks in verse 27 about being "disqualified for the prize," he is not suggesting the possibility that he might lose his salvation. Instead he focuses on the fearful possibility that he might forfeit eternal reward by failing to fulfill God's purposes for his life.

Like Paul, we must be fiercely determined to run in such a way that we will win the prize! The serious contestant in a race does not run with his luggage. Anything weighing us down must be eliminated. Unnecessary burdens and sins such as worries, guilt and unforgiveness hinder our ability to run effectively. The race is real, and our Lord will place crowns of victory on those who win.

> Let us lay aside every weight, and the sin which so easily ensnares us, and let us run with endurance the race that is set before us, looking unto Jesus, the author and finisher of our faith. . . .
>
> Hebrews 12:1–2, NKJV

Don't Compare Yourself with Others

In 1990 the best collegiate track athletes gathered for the National Collegiate Athletic Association championships. As the runner leading in the men's 1500-meter finals approached the finish line, he looked to his left. Seeing he was still ahead with only a couple of meters to go, he raised his hands in celebration. But because he failed to lean forward to hit the tape, a runner on his right edged him out for the victory. Looking to his side cost him the national championship.

Turning to the side to compare ourselves with others can hinder us from winning an eternal reward. We are deceived when we think that how we compare to others really matters. God will not judge us by comparing us to others; He will judge us relative to what He has given us: "To whom much is given, from him much will be required" (Luke 12:48, NKJV).

We cannot evaluate ourselves correctly by comparing ourselves to others because we have different gifts and different callings. Each of us must be faithful with whatever we have been given.

Jesus spoke to Peter about this issue in John 21:20–22. He told Peter to follow Him, but Peter was distracted by someone else.

> Peter turned and saw [John] following them. . . . When Peter saw him, he said to Jesus, "Lord, what about this man?" Jesus said to him, ". . . What is that to you? Follow me!"

152

Peter was not to concern himself with John's obedience, only with his own.

In the same way, if we want to win the prize, we need to follow Christ diligently, regardless of what anyone else does. Jonathan Edwards, eighteenth-century theologian and preacher, held just such a commitment:

> Resolved: To follow God with all my heart.
> Resolved also: Whether others do or not, I will.[1]

So Get Ready!

Jesus says:

> "Behold, I am coming soon! My reward is with me, and I will give to everyone according to what he has done."
>
> Revelation 22:12, NIV

We hope this book has increased your desire to live completely for Jesus Christ, and that you have found these truths as stunning and life-changing as we have. The Lord's desire is to say to you on that Day, "Well done, good and faithful servant! Enter into the joy of your Master!"

Please be sure to read Appendix B! It is the account of General William Booth, founder of the Salvation Army, who told of a powerful vision he received about an uncommitted Christian who dies and comes face to face with Jesus Christ.

Appendix A

ARE YOU GOOD ENOUGH TO GET TO HEAVEN?

The words startled the young man as he stood at the bedside of his dying father: "Son, I'm worried that I might not go to heaven when I die."

"But Dad, I don't know anyone who's lived a better life than you! You're the best man I know."

The troubled father replied, "I just don't know if it's enough."

Can We Know for Sure
We Will Go to Heaven When We Die?

One of the most fascinating stories in the Bible sheds light on this question. Numbers 21:5–9 tells about an entire nation of people who rebelled against God and, as a result, were overrun with poisonous snakes. As they began to die from snakebites, they admitted their sin of rebelliousness and asked their leader, Moses, to pray for them.

When Moses prayed, God gave him some unusual instructions: Make a brass snake and lift it high on a pole. If those who have been bitten will look up at the brass snake, they will recover.

Sure enough, everyone who looked, lived!

When Jesus Christ, God's Son, was on earth, He retold the story of the brass snake. Then He revealed that the brass snake actually represented Him. Jesus said, "As Moses lifted up the serpent in the wilderness, so must the Son of man be lifted up, that whoever believes in him may have eternal life" (John 3:14–15). Jesus was speaking of His eventual crucifixion, when he was cruelly nailed to a Roman executioner's cross and lifted high in the air while He died.

To rescue us from the deadly effects of our own sin, God sent His Son to die in our place. The Bible explains it this way: "For God so loved the world that he gave his only Son, that whoever believes in him should not perish but have eternal life" (John 3:16).

Why doesn't everyone look to Christ and accept God's free gift of forgiveness and eternal life? One reason is that many people do not know they have a problem. They do not see their need. It is as if they have received a deadly snakebite but do not realize it.

Another reason people do not look to Christ and accept the free gift of eternal life is that they look elsewhere for salvation, especially to themselves. They believe the idea that "good people go to heaven and bad people go to hell," and then they try to make themselves good enough to get to heaven. Their trust is in *themselves.*

No One Is Good Enough to Get to Heaven!

Jesus once told a story "to some who were confident of their own righteousness" (Luke 18:9, NIV). In the story a man boasts in prayer, "God, I thank thee that I am not like other men. . . .

I fast twice a week, I give tithes of all that I get" (verses 11–12). This man is impressed with himself. He deludes himself into thinking that he is right with God, but Jesus assures us that he is not.

Many people today make the same mistake. They think they will get to heaven because of their own righteousness. "I'm basically a good person," they say. "I haven't killed anyone. I'm better than most people. I've done more good than bad. I attend church. I . . . I . . . I . . . !"

It's all *self*-righteousness. If we rely on our own goodness to get us to heaven, *we will never get there.* Jesus Christ says, "I am the way, and the truth, and the life; no one comes to the Father, but by me" (John 14:6). The Bible tells us what Jesus did for us and why: "Christ also died for sins once for all, the righteous for the unrighteous, that he might bring us to God" (1 Peter 3:18). As far as salvation is concerned, one look at Christ is worth more than a million looks at self!

But self-righteous people are too proud to admit they need a Savior. To them the cross of Christ seems irrelevant. They neglect or refuse God's offer to rescue them from their sins because they think they are just fine on their own. They are trusting in their own righteousness.

Good People Do Not Go to Heaven; Only Forgiven People Do

Jesus wants us to trust in Him because nothing else is capable of bringing us to God. Not good deeds. Not religion. Not anything.

God's two greatest commandments are to "love the Lord your God with all your heart, and with all your soul, and with all your mind, and with all your strength" and to "love your neighbor as yourself" (Mark 12:30–31). Who can claim to have kept these commandments perfectly, even for a day?

157

Many of us do not realize we are in danger, but God's assessment of our situation is summed up in the following verses:

All have sinned and fall short of the glory of God.

Romans 3:23

The wages of sin is death [eternal separation from God], but the free gift of God is eternal life in Christ Jesus our Lord.

Romans 6:23

We can place our trust in Jesus as payment for our sins, or we can trust in ourselves and fall short. Jesus died to pay sin's penalty for us and rose again to make a relationship with God possible. Now God can justly offer forgiveness to those who would otherwise spend eternity in hell. Good people do not go to heaven; only *forgiven* people do.

It's Your Choice

You are being invited to enter into the most loving relationship you will ever experience. But God gave you free will. He did not make you a puppet who would be forced to love Him back. He gives you the freedom to follow Him or to go your own way.

Do you agree with God that you need the forgiveness He provides through His Son? Would you like to receive forgiveness and enter into a right relationship with God today? Here is a prayer you can pray right now:

Lord Jesus, thank You for loving me so much that You were willing to be punished on the cross for my sins so I could be forgiven. I open my heart to You and invite you to be my Savior. I acknowledge that You know what is best for me. Teach me to please You in every part of my life. Thank You for Your forgiveness and for the gift of eternal life.

Appendix B

THE VISION OF WILLIAM BOOTH

This is the account of a remarkable and alarming vision received by General William Booth, founder of the Salvation Army. General Booth was outstandingly courageous and zealous in his service for God and others. This vision intensified his future service and became a life-changing admonition to thousands.[1]

I had a very strange vision the other day. And I have been greatly perplexed as to whether or not I should tell it to others. . . .

In my vision I thought that so far as the world was concerned, Agur's prayer was answered in regard to me, for I had neither poverty nor riches. All my wants were supplied. I had leisure, and friends, and home, and all that was necessary to make me happy. . . .

We visited together at each other's homes, joined in amusements, business, politics and many other things. In short, we bought and sold, and married, and acted as though the world we were in were going to last forever.

In this vision I was one who was active in religious activities. In fact, I considered myself to be quite a shining light. I always attended church on Sunday and I taught in the Sunday School. Now and then, though not very often, I visited the sick. And in addition to these good deeds I gave a little money to support Christian work.

In all this I was quite sincere. I had no idea of playing the hypocrite. It's true that I didn't stop to consider what Christianity really was, although I talked freely enough about it at times, and pitied people who didn't profess to be Christians.

I seldom, if ever, considered what Jesus Christ required. Nor was I very concerned about the lost, although I heard these matters occasionally discussed in my presence. I had gotten into a definite rut in thought and action and profession. And I went on from day to day, hoping that everything would turn out all right in the end.

But in my vision I thought that without any apparent warning a dangerous fever seized me. I became terribly sick all of a sudden. In fact, in just a few hours I was brought to the very brink of death. This was serious business indeed. Everyone about me was in great confusion. And those who loved me were paralyzed with fear.

Some took action. The proper medicines were administered. There were consultations among several physicians. And the members of my family hurried to my side from far and near. Friends and acquaintances came.

I was given the best medical care possible—but all proved in vain.

I could feel that the medicines weren't helping. And yet I didn't feel anything very much. I don't know whether this was because of the suddenness of the sickness or the deadening character of the narcotics which the physicians gave me. But strangely enough I seemed to be the least disturbed person in the place.

I felt as though I were in a dream. I knew I was ill—dangerously ill—because a relative had insisted on my being informed of my real condition. And yet I was not disturbed about the fact. I thought I would recover. Most people do, I suppose, until the hand of death is actually upon them.

And if I did not recover, I had no reason to be terribly concerned, because, wasn't I a Christian? Hadn't I been converted? Didn't I believe the Bible? Why should I fear?

And wasn't I continually hearing hymns being sung and prayers offered that I might be restored to health, and if not, that I might pass away without suffering, and have a good time of it in heaven?

But even so, disquieting thoughts did cross my mind—because I couldn't keep out questions that kept arising as to whether I had truly followed Jesus Christ and had done my duty to a perishing world with my time and influence, and money and family. And questions would come and go that were very difficult indeed to answer. Yet it was all in a dreamy way. How could it be otherwise, with the burning fever lapping up the vital current, and my brain all benumbed, and my energies laid prostrate?

So when I complained that I didn't have much joy or assurance, I quite naturally agreed readily to the suggestion that my condition prevented this. . . .

One thing I could do, and that I did. I cast myself, with what force of soul I had left, on the mercy of my Savior. . . . Meanwhile a strange faintness seized me. I lost consciousness.

Entrance into Heaven

My next sensation was altogether beyond description. It was a thrill of a new and celestial existence. I was in heaven.

After the first feeling of surprise had somewhat subsided, I looked around me, and took in the situation. It was way beyond anything of earth—positively delightful. . . . No human

161

eyes ever beheld such perfection, such beauty. No earthly ear ever heard such music. . . . At first I was swallowed up with a sort of ecstatic intoxication, which feeling was immediately enhanced by the consciousness that I was safe, saved, to suffer and sin no more.

And then, suddenly, a new set of feelings began to creep over me. Strange as it may seem, I felt somewhat lonely and a little sad, even in the midst of this infinite state of bliss. Because up to this moment I was alone. Not one of the bright beings who were soaring and singing in the bright ether above me, nor the ones who were hastening hither and thither, as though bent upon some high mission, had spoken to me or approached me.

I was alone in heaven! Then, in a still stranger and mysterious way, I appeared to feel in myself a sort of unfitness for the society of those pure beings who were sailing around me in indescribable loveliness. How could it be? Had I come there by mistake? Was I not counted worthy of this glorious inheritance? It was indeed a mystery.

An Evaluation of My Life

My thoughts went back to earth. And all before me, as though unfolded by an angel's hand, the record of my past life was unrolled before my eyes. What a record it was! I glanced over it. And in a glance I seemed to master its entire contents—so rapidly, indeed, that I became conscious of a marvelous quickening of my intellectual powers. I realized that I could take in and understand in a moment what would have required a day with my poor, darkened faculties on earth.

With my quickened mind, I saw, to my delight, at that very first glance, that this register of my earthly existence—the Divine biography of my life—contained no record of any misdeeds before my conversion. Indeed, that part of my life seemed to be very much of a blank. I further perceived that neither was there any record of the sins I had done since that time. It was as though some friendly hand had gone through the roll and blotted out the record of the evil doings of my life. This was very gratifying. I felt like shouting praises to God, who had delivered me from the pain of having these things staring me in the face in this beautiful, holy land, among all these holy beings, where it seemed to me that the very memory of sin would defile.

Nevertheless, a further glance at my record appalled me, for there was written therein—leaving out, as I have said, the sins of commission—the exact daily record of the whole of my past life! In fact, it went much deeper, because it described in full detail the object for which I had lived. It recorded my thoughts and feelings and actions—how and for what I had employed my time, my money, my influence, and all the other talents and gifts which God had entrusted me with to spend for His glory and for the salvation of the lost.

Every chapter of this record carried my thoughts back to the condition of the world I had left. And there came up before my eyes a vivid picture of its hatred for God, its rejection of Christ, its wickedness, with all the wretchedness and destitution and abomination. It utterly appalled me. Also into my ears there came a hurricane of cursing and blasphemy, and a wail of anguish and woe that stunned me.

I had seen these sights and had heard these sounds before—not too often, it is true, because I had hid myself from them. But now they blinded and stunned me. They appeared a million times blacker and more vile, more wretched and piteous, than they had ever seemed before!

I felt like putting my hands before my eyes, and my fingers in my ears to shut these things out from sight and hearing, so intensely real and present did they seem. They wrung my soul with sorrow and self-reproach, because on the "Record of Memory" I saw how I had occupied myself during the few years which I had been allowed to live amidst all these miseries, after Jesus Christ had called me to be His soldier. I was reminded how, instead of fighting His battles, instead of saving souls by bringing them to His feet, and so preparing them for admission into this lovely place, I had been on the contrary, intent on earthly things, selfishly seeking my own, spending my life in practical unbelief, disloyalty and disobedience.

I felt sick at heart. Oh, if at that moment I could have crept out of the "land of pure delight" about which I had sung so much in the past, and could have gone back to the world of darkness, sin and misery, which I had just left—if I could but spend another lifetime among the lost and dying, and truly follow my Lord!

But that could not be. My opportunities of earth were past. Heaven must now be my dwelling forever. And contradictory as it may seem, this thought filled my soul with unspeakable regret.

And then came another thought, more wild than any that had gone before it. . . . It was this: Would it be possible for me to obtain permission to go back to the world, to that very part of it from which I had come, clothed in some human form, and live my earthly life over again—live it in a manner worthy of my profession, worthy of my Christ and my opportunity? Could this be?

If at that moment an answer in the affirmative had been brought to me, I would have gladly given up my heavenly blessedness. I would have gladly undergone ages of hardship, ignominy, poverty and pain. I would have given up a million dollars in money. Yes, I would have gladly given a world, if it had been mine to give! But I could see no hope for a second probation. What was to be done?

Questioned by a Man

I had not been musing in this way for many seconds, for thoughts appeared to flow with remarkable rapidity, when, quick as a lightning flash, one of those bright inhabitants, which I had watched floating far off in the clouds of glory, descended and stood before my astonished gaze.

I can never forget the awe-struck feelings with which I beheld this heavenly being. Describe the shape and features and bearing of this noble form I cannot, and will not attempt it. He was at the same time angelic and human, earthly and yet celestial. I discerned therefore at a glance that he was one of the "blood-washed multitude" who had "come out of the great tribulations of earth." I not only judged from a certain majestic appearance which he bore, but from instinct I felt that the being before me was a man, a redeemed and glorified man.

He looked at me. And I could not keep from returning his gaze. I could never have believed the human face divine could ever bear so grand a stamp of dignity and charm.

But far beyond the entrancing loveliness of those celestial features was the expression which filled his total countenance, and shone through those eyes that were gazing upon me. It was as though that face was only a sunlit window, through which I could see into the depths of the pure, kindly and tender soul within.

I don't know how I looked to my beautiful visitor. I don't know what form I had. I had not seen myself in a mirror since I had taken on immortality for mortality.

It was evident that he had a deep interest in me. But it was an interest which seemed to bring sadness to him. His features seemed to me to grow almost sorrowful as I sat there with my eyes fixed on him in a fascinated spell.

He spoke first. Had he not done so, I could never have summoned courage to address him. His voice was soft and musical, and fitted well with the seriousness of his bearing. I understood him almost before I heard his words, although I cannot tell now what language he spoke. I suppose it was the universal language of heaven.

This was the substance of what he said: My arrival was known throughout a certain district of the celestial regions, where were gathered the ransomed ones who had come from the earthly neighborhood where I had lived. The tidings of my arrival had been flashed through the heavenly telephone, which spoke not in one ear only, but in every ear in that particular region. My name had been whispered in every hillside and echoed in every valley, and had been spoken in every room of every mansion. It had been proclaimed from every tower and pinnacle of the stupendous temple in which these glorified saints day and night present their worship to the great Father.

All who had known me on earth, all who had any knowledge of my family, my opportunities for helping forward the Kingdom of Christ, whom they worshipped and adored, were burning to see me and hear me tell of the victories I had won and the souls I had blessed while on earth. And all were especially anxious to hear if I had been the means of bringing salvation to the loved ones they had left behind.

All this was poured upon my soul. I didn't know which way to look. Again and again I remembered my life of ease and comfort. What could I say? How could I appear with the record of my life before these waiting ones? What was there in it except a record of self-gratification? I had no martyr stories to tell. I had sacrificed nothing worth naming on earth, much less in heaven, for His dear sake!

My mind was running in this direction when I think my visitor must have discovered something of what I was thinking, and felt pity for me. Seeing my consternation, he spoke again.

"Where you find yourself is not actually heaven," he said, "but only its forecourt, a sort of outer circle. Presently the Lord Himself, with a great procession of His chosen ones, will come to take you into the Celestial City itself. There is where your residence will be if He deems you worthy; that is, if your conduct on the battlefield below has pleased Him.

"Meanwhile, I have obtained permission to come and speak to you concerning a soul who is very dear to me. I understand he lives in the neighborhood where you recently lived, and from which have just come. Our knowledge of the affairs of earth is, for our own sakes, limited, but now and then we are permitted to get a glimpse.

"Can you," he said, "tell me anything about my son? He was my only son. I loved him dearly. I loved him too much. I spoiled him when a child! He had his own way. He grew up willful, passionate and disobedient. And my example didn't help him."

Here a cloud for a moment came over the beautiful brow, but vanished as quickly as it came. . . . He, the father, had been rescued, washed, regenerated. He had learned to fight for souls, and had won many to the blood-stained banner. Then he had suddenly been taken in death by an accident at his work and was taken to heaven.

"And now," he added, "where is my boy? Give me tidings of my boy! He lived near you, and had business dealings with you. What did you do for him? Is there hope? Tell me what his feelings are today."

He stopped speaking. My heart sank within me. What could I say? I knew the boy. The story of the father's death and his prodigal son had been told me. I had never spoken one serious word to the boy about his soul or about his Savior. I had been busy about other things. And now, what could I say to his father, who stood before me? I was speechless!

The cloud that I had noticed before again came over the face of my visitor, but with a dark shadow this time. He must have guessed the truth. He looked at me with a look in which I felt that disappointment to himself and pity for me were combined. He then spread his wings and soared away.

I was so intently gazing after his retreating form that I hadn't noticed a second fair being, who had descended from above, and who now occupied the place abandoned only a moment before by my last visitor.

I turned and looked upon the newcomer. This was a spirit of the same class, of the same ransomed multitude who once were dwellers on earth. There was a dignity of bearing, the

But in this case there was a beauty (which I could never have imagined) of more delicate and enthralling mold.

Beautiful as I thought my first visitor to be, more beautiful than conception or dream of earth could be, yet here was a beauty that surpassed it . . . My former visitor I have said was a glorified man—this one was evidently the glorified form of a woman. . . .

The fair creature . . . evidently wished to speak to me on some matter of great importance.

She told me her name. I had heard it on earth. She was a widow who had struggled through great difficulties. Her husband's death had resulted in her conversion to Christ. Converted, she had given herself up unreservedly to fight for the Lord. Her children had been her first care. They had all been saved, and were fighting for God, except one.

The mention of that name brought the same saddening cloud on her lovely face which had dimmed the bright face of my first visitor. But the cloud vanished almost as soon as it came. That one, that unsaved one, was a girl who had been her mother's delight. She had grown up beautiful, the village pride, but alas! had gone astray. It was the old story of wrong, and of being seduced into evil ways. And then of utter abandonment to that way of life, and all the consequent train of miseries.

I listened. I had known some of the sad story on earth, but I had turned away from hearing any more about it as being "no concern of mine." Little did I ever think that I would be confronted with it in heaven!

And now the bright spirit turned those eyes on me that, beaming with love and concern, were more beautiful than ever. She said again: "My daughter lived near you. You know her. Have you saved her? I don't know much about her, but I do know that one earnest and determined effort would save her, and win her to Christ."

And then again she asked me, "Have you saved my child?"

I must have cried out in agony. I know I put my hands over my eyes, because I could no longer bear to meet her intent look, which now turned to one of pity for me.

How long she continued to look on me, with an expression of concern almost greater than she had shown for her lost child, I do not know. But when I uncovered my eyes, she was gone, and the silvery sheen of her white wings marked her out to my seeking eyes like a speck on the distant blue.

Then I cried out, "Oh, my God, is this heaven? Will these questionings go on forever? Will the meanness and selfishness of my past life haunt me throughout eternity? What shall I do? Can I not go back to earth, and do something to redeem myself from this wretched sense of unworthiness? Can I not live my life over again?"

This question had hardly passed through my mind when there was another rush of wings, and down beside me alighted another form. . . . He introduced himself much in the same way as my former visitors. He had been a great singer, but was awakened and won to Christ only a short while back. Having had much forgiven, he had loved much. All his desire after his conversion was to get free from the entanglements of business and to devote himself a living sacrifice to the saving of men.

When just on the threshold of the realization of his wish, he had been sent to heaven. And here he was, a spirit of glory and joy, coming to inquire of me concerning the church group among whom he had labored, and of the crowd of companions he had left behind. Was I acquainted with his little church? Their place of worship was near my place of business. Had I helped them in their difficulties, and in their service and testimony for Christ? Had I done anything for his old mates, who were drinking and cursing their way to hell? He had died with prayers for them on his lips. Had I stopped them on their way to ruin?

Again I could not speak. What could I say? I knew his church. But I had never given them any encouragement or help. I knew of the hovels in which his old mates lived, and the dens of hell in which they spent their time and money. But I had been too busy, or too proud, or too cowardly, to seek them out with the message of the Savior's love.

I was utterly speechless. He guessed my feelings, I suppose, because with a look of sympathy he left in sadness—at least in as much sadness as is possible in heaven.

The King's Procession

As for myself, I was in anguish—strange as it may appear, considering I was in heaven. But so it was. Wondering whether there was not some comfort for me, I involuntarily looked around. And I saw a marvelous phenomenon on the horizon at a great distance. All that part of the heavens appeared to be filled with a brilliant light, surpassing the blaze of a thousand suns at noonday. And yet there was no blinding glare making it difficult to gaze upon, as is the case with our own sun when it shines in its glory. Here was a brilliance far surpassing anything that could be imagined, and yet I could look upon it with pleasure.

As I continued to gaze, wondering what it could be, it appeared to come a little closer. Then I realized it was coming in my direction.

And now I could distinctly hear the sound of music. The distance was a great many miles, after the measurement of earth, but the atmosphere was so clear, and I found my eyesight so strong, that I could easily see objects at a distance which, on earth, would have required a powerful telescope.

The sound came closer. It was music, beyond question— and such music as I had never heard before. But there was a strange commingling of other sounds which all together made a marvelous melody, made up, as I afterwards discovered, by the strains that came from the multitude of musicians, and the shouts and songs that proceeded from innumerable voices.

This phenomenon was approaching rapidly. But my curiosity was so strongly aroused to know what it was, that a few minutes seemed an age.

Finally I was able to make out what it was. It was astounding! But who could describe it? The whole firmament was filled, as it were, with innumerable forms, each of beauty and dignity, far surpassing those with whom I had already made an acquaintance. Here was a representative portion of the aristocracy of heaven accompanying the King, who came to welcome into the heaven of heavens the spirits of men and women who had escaped from earth, who had fought the good fight, who had kept the faith, and had overcome in the conflict as He had overcome.

I stood filled with awe and wonder. Could it be possible? Was I at last actually to see my Lord and be welcomed by Him? In the thought of this rapture I forgot the sorrow that only a moment before had reigned in my heart, and my whole nature swelled with expectation and delight.

And now the procession was upon me. I had seen some of the pageants of earth—displays that required the power of mighty monarchs, and the wealth of great cities and nations to create—but they were each or all combined, as the feeble light of a candle to a tropical sun in comparison with the tremendous scene which now spread itself before my astonished eyes.

On it came. I had sprung up from my reclining position, and then had fallen prostrate as the first rank of these shining heavenly spirits neared me. Each one looked in himself, to my untutored eyes, like a god, so far as greatness and power could be expressed by the outward appearance of any being.

Rank after rank swept past me. Each turned his eyes upon me, or seemed to do so. I could not help feeling that I was somewhat an object of pity to them all. Perhaps it was my own feelings that made me imagine this. But it certainly appeared to me as though these noble beings regarded me as a fearful, cowardly soul, who had only cared for his own interests on earth, and had come up there with the same selfish motives.

On they came. Thousands passed me, yet there appeared to me to be no diminishment in the numbers yet to come. I looked at the procession as it stretched backwards, but my eyes could see no end to it. There must have been millions. It was indeed a "multitude that no man could number."

All were praising God, either in hymns expressive of adoration and worship, or by recounting, in songs of rapture, the mighty victories which they had witnessed on earth—or describing some wonderful work they had seen elsewhere.

And now, the great, central glory and attraction of the splendid procession was at hand.

I gathered this from the still more dignified character of beings who now swept by, the heavier crash of music, and the louder shouts of exultation which came pealing from all around.

I was right, and before I could prepare my spirit for the visitation, it was upon me. The King was here! In the center of circling hosts—which rose tier above tier into the blue vault above, turning on Him their millions of eyes, lustrous with the love they bore Him—I beheld the celestial form of Him who died for me upon the cross. The procession halted. Then at a word of command, they formed up instantly in three sides of a square in front of me, the King standing in the center immediately opposite the spot where I had prostrated myself.

What a sight that was! Worth toiling a lifetime to behold it! Nearest to the King were the patriarchs and apostles of ancient times. Next, rank after rank, came the holy martyrs who had died for Him. Then came the army of warriors who had fought for Him in every part of the world.

And around and about, above and below, I beheld myriads and myriads of spirits who were never heard of on earth outside their own neighborhood, or beyond their own times, who, with self-denying zeal and untiring toil, had labored to extend God's Kingdom and to save the souls of men. And encircling the gorgeous scene, above, beneath, around, hovered glittering angelic beings who had kept their first estate—proud, it seemed to me, to minister to the happiness and exaltation of these redeemed out of the poor world from which I came.

Face to Face with the King

I was bewildered by the scene. The songs, the music, the shouts of the multitude that came like the roar of a thousand cataracts, echoed and re-echoed through the sunlit mountains. And the magnificent and endless array of happy spirits ravished my senses with passionate delight. All at once, however, I remembered myself, and was reminded of the High Presence before Whom I was bowed, and lifting up my eyes I beheld Him gazing upon me.

What a look it was! It was not pain, and yet it was not pleasure. It was not anger, and yet it was not approval. Anyway, I felt that in that face, so inexpressibly admirable and glorious, there was yet no welcome for me. I had felt this in the faces of my previous visitors. I felt it again in the Lord's.

That face, that Divine face, seemed to say to me, for language was not needed to convey to the very depths of my soul what His feelings were to me: "Thou wilt feel thyself little in harmony with these, once the companions of My tribulations and now of My glory, who counted not their lives dear unto themselves, in order that they might bring honor to Me and salvation to men." And He gave a look of admiration at the host of apostles and martyrs and warriors gathered around Him.

Oh, that look of Jesus! I felt that to have one such loving recognition—it would be worth dying a hundred deaths at the stake. It would be worth being torn asunder by wild beasts. The angelic escort felt it, too, for their responsive burst of praise and song shook the very skies and the ground on which I lay.

Then the King turned His eyes on me again. How I wished that some mountain would fall upon me and hide me forever from His presence! But I wished in vain. Some invisible and irresistible force compelled me to look up, and my eyes met His once more. I felt, rather than heard, Him saying to me in words that engraved themselves as fire upon my brain:

"Go back to earth. I will give thee another opportunity. Prove thyself worthy of My name. Show to the world that thou possessest My Spirit by doing My works, and becoming, on My behalf, a savior of men. Thou shalt return hither when thou hast finished the battle, and I will give thee a place in My conquering train, and a share in My glory."

What I felt under that look and those words, no heart or mind could possibly describe. They were mingled feelings. First came the unutterable anguish arising out of the full realization that I had wasted my life, that it had been a life squandered on the paltry ambitions and trifling pleasures of earth—while it might have been filled and sown with deeds that would have produced a never-ending harvest of heavenly fruit. My life could have won for me the approval of heaven's King, and made me worthy to be the companion of these glorified heroes.

But combined with this self-reproach there was a gleam of hope. My earnest desire to return to earth was to be granted. . . . I could have the privilege of living my life over again. True, it was a high responsibility, but Jesus would be with me. His Spirit would enable me. And in my heart I felt ready to face it.

The cloud of shining ones had vanished. The music was silent. I closed my eyes and gave myself over, body, soul, and spirit, to the disposal of my Savior—to live, not for my own salvation, but for the glory of my Christ, and for the salvation of the world. And then and there, the same blessed voice of my King stole over my heart, as He promised that His presence should go with me back to earth, and make me more than a conqueror through His blood.

(*This Was Your Life!* video information can be found on p. 191.)

STUDY GUIDE

Questions for Group Discussion and Personal Reflection

Chapter 1: Encountering the Christ of Revelation

1. How would you have answered Ed's question: "Have you ever thought much about the Judgment Seat of Christ?" Why do you think many Christians have not given much thought to it? What do you think would happen to the Church if they did?

2. What three adjectives would you use to describe Lily Shipton's Christian life? What about Todd's? What about yours?

3. Is there a Lily Shipton in your life whom you should thank? If so, who? In what ways did this person impact your life?

4. Is there someone you could be a Lily Shipton to? If so, who? What are some practical things you can do to encourage that person in his or her walk with Christ?

5. Do you think God will reward Lily Shipton for the extra fruit produced by Rick Howard's life because of her influence on him?

6. What is wood, hay and stubble in your life? Are you willing to relinquish those areas to God so He can enrich your life beyond anything you have ever dreamed? Is there anything holding you back? Ask God to do a deep work in your heart as you read the chapters that follow.

Chapter 2: Take Heed How You Build

1. If you were to die today and God asked you, "Why should I let you into My heaven?" how would you respond?

2. Does your answer to question 1 show that your faith is in Christ, in yourself, or in something else?

3. Would God be able to accept the most moral person in the world based on that person's own righteousness? Give one or two Bible references that back up your answer.

4. Does the life you lead prove you genuinely believe you will someday give account to the living God?

5. If you knew Christ was returning exactly one year from today, what would you do to prepare yourself for His return? What (if anything) hinders you from doing those things now?

Chapter 3: How Do We Bear Much Fruit?

1. What kind of fruit do you want God to bear in your life?

2. What do farmers do to increase the fruitfulness of their fields? What spiritual parallels do you see?

3. What is at the root of getting down on oneself? What is the cure?

4. What did Jeremiah do to find release from discouragement and depression (see Lamentations 3:19–25)? What is one circumstance you are experiencing that requires calling

to mind God's truth in order to find hope? What is an example of a lie the enemy has used against you? With what corresponding truth can you counter this lie?

5. Do you keep a journal of all that God reveals to you? If not, start one today! If you already keep such a journal, do you review it periodically and "chew the cud"?

6. Does God's Word guide you like the plane's instruments guide an experienced pilot? What verses do you apply to your daily life? (See Ephesians 4:32; Philippians 2:3–4; 1 Peter 5:7.)

7. In what ways have you been relying on your feelings more than the truths of God's Word? Prepare index cards with Scriptures that speak specifically to those areas. Review these Scriptures each day until your heart is established in the truth.

Chapter 4: Lay Up Treasures in Heaven

1. What practical things can you do to keep temporal concerns from crowding out the eternal?

2. What are some ways we can lay up treasures in heaven? What role do our motives play?

3. Before reading this book, did you think seeking heavenly rewards is selfish or immature? What do you think now? What are some facts about the rewards that render them desirable by unselfish, mature believers?

4. With regard to the lightbulb analogy, how brightly is your life shining, and why? (When I get to heaven, I don't want to be a nightlight, do you?)

Chapter 5: The Ultimate Test

1. If your life on earth were to end today, would you approach the Judgment Seat with confidence or shame? Why?

2. Find an extended, uninterrupted time before the Lord and imagine yourself in the role of George Bailey in "It's a Won-

derful Life." Ask God to show you some of your life's lasting, positive impact on others. Ask Him to show you areas in which you are building castles in the sand. Ask Him to impress deeply upon your heart and mind the great significance of each moment of life and help you strategize accordingly.

3. What kind of person is able to have a deep, positive impact on the lives of others? How can you develop these traits in yourself?

4. Identify times in your own life when one person's kindness toward you inspired you to be kind to someone else.

5. What act of kindness can you perform during the next 24 hours? Knock down some dominoes!

6. List some of the talents God has given you for advancing His Kingdom. Which of your talents have you "put to work" and which have you kept hidden?

Chapter 6: Ultimate Success

1. Give some examples of ways people spend their lives accomplishing goals as eternally useless as touching the painted lines with their feet.

2. What is your rudder set on?

3. What are some of the things in your life that might alert you to the presence of self-gratification as a driving purpose? What might alert you to the presence of self-preservation? Take some time alone with the Lord and ask Him to illuminate any "purposes of the heart" from which you need to repent.

4. Have you ever been afraid to repent because you think your plans are better than God's plans? Explain. (Note: 2 Corinthians 7:10 says "repentance . . . brings no regret." Because God is so good, no one in the history of the world has ever regretted repenting.)

5. First Corinthians 5:9 says we should make it our aim to please the Lord, but Ephesians 5:10 takes us a step further. It

says "try to learn what is pleasing to the Lord." Consider studying the Scriptures to find out how to please Him. Here are some references to help you get started:

Hebrews 13:16
Colossians 3:20
Ezekiel 18:23
1 Timothy 5:4
1 Thessalonians 4:1, 3–6

Chapter 7: Take Responsibility—But Not Too Much!

1. Moses blamed the people for his not being allowed to enter the Promised Land (see Deuteronomy 1:37), but notice how God assesses the situation in Numbers 27:14 and Deuteronomy 32:51. Is there sin in your life you are blaming on someone else? Is there sin in your life you are blaming on bad circumstances? Knowing you are ultimately responsible to obey God regardless of what others do and regardless of circumstances, is there a sin you need to turn from right now?

2. Do you have any goals for yourself that are outside of your control?

3. Describe a time when you felt frustrated or angry. Identify a blocked goal that caused the frustration. How could you have changed your goal? What new, proper goal might you have adopted in its place?

4. Describe a time when you were nervous. Were you trying to control something outside of your control? How could you have adjusted your goal?

5. What does the chapter say should be our "one overriding goal in life"? Explain in your own words why this goal cannot be blocked.

6. What lesson do we find in the life of Joseph concerning how to deal with bad circumstances and mistreatment? To what situation in your own life could you apply this lesson?

Chapter 8: The Fear of Man

1. We are warned in Proverbs 29:25 that "the fear of man lays a snare." Why do you think so many of us are driven by the question, What do people think of me? What are some of the traps we can fall into by worrying about what people think of us?

2. In light of Matthew 6:1–2, explain the statement "God will not reward all good deeds."

3. Explain how the fear of man is a hindrance to genuine love.

4. Once when I was giving a final exam, it was obvious to me that one of my students was cheating. When he turned in his paper, I told him I had seen him looking at another student's answers. He denied it (which didn't surprise me). However, when I compared the two exams, there was no correlation between the answers! I was convinced he was cheating, but I was wrong. Aren't you glad I'm not your judge? What does Isaiah 11:3–4 say about how the Messiah will judge?

5. Have you ever been falsely accused? What emotions did you experience? How did you respond? What is the biblical response?

Chapter 9: Developing a Servant's Heart

1. In what area of your life have you had the most difficulty casting your cares upon God? Will you accept the truth that no care is "uncastable"? Will you trust in God's goodness and wisdom?

2. Ask the Holy Spirit to expose any cares you have been carrying around. Take some time now to cast all your cares on Him.

3. Is becoming a doormat for others to walk on a loving thing to do? (Is that seeking their highest good?)

4. Read Mark 10:37–45. Does Jesus indicate that everyone will be equally close to God in heaven? What is the basis for greatness in His Kingdom?

5. What are three ways to develop the mindset of a servant? Choose one and consider how you can implement it in your life during the next 24 hours.

6. If you were in the hospital, what would you like someone to do for you? Can you do that for someone else?

7. What causes most depression? According to John 15:11–12, what is the secret to walking in joy?

8. What wrong mindset causes loneliness? What is the cure?

9. What symptoms of stage fright have you experienced? What improper goals cause stage fright? What proper goal should we adopt to cure it?

Chapter 10: Stay Out of His Chair!

1. Have you ever found yourself in God's chair? What happened?

2. Think of a person you have judged. When you have a judgmental, critical spirit, does it ever produced good fruit or constructive change in the life of the other person? (See James 1:20.) Discuss the difference between judgmentalism and "speaking the truth in love" (Ephesians 4:15).

3. Can you identify biblical passages in which someone judged God (looking down on Him or speaking against Him)? Can you identify a time in which you have judged God?

4. Have you at times doubted God's goodness or kindness? Prepare some flash cards with Scriptures on them so you can

meditate on truths about God's wonderful character. Here are some references to help you get started:

Psalm 145:17
Psalm 34:8
Psalm 136

5. Memorize and meditate on the second half of Isaiah 66:2. How does pride interfere with our taking God's Word seriously?

Chapter 11: The Fear of the Lord Is a Fountain of Life

1. Are there areas in your life in which you are afraid of God's will being done? What do you think He might do in those areas? What would it take for you not to be afraid?

2. Did your family talk about God when you were small? How was the subject of God handled in your home when you were growing up?

3. Did your family teach you to fear God? If so, was your fear of God healthy or unhealthy?

4. How has your view of God changed during your lifetime?

5. What are the benefits of a proper fear of the Lord? Why is the fear of the Lord called "the beginning of wisdom"? Why is the fear of the Lord called "the fountain of life"?

Chapter 12: Pleasing God in Your Work

1. If you stood before God right this minute, would He be pleased with your workplace motivation? Why or why not?

2. Many Christians seem to separate their work life from their spiritual life. Why do you think that happens?

3. Think about your work. What are the thieves of motivation you face there? How can Colossians 3:22–24 help to bring joy into your work life?

4. What keeps ordinary, secular work from being ordinary and secular?

5. What are the characteristics of menpleasers versus Godpleasers?

Chapter 13: Seizing the Time

1. Has God given you a vision for your life? If so, what gifts and talents has He empowered you with to accomplish this vision?

2. Sometimes people yearn to bloom where they are not planted. What are some ways you can bloom where you are planted?

3. What is the most helpful time-management tip you got out of this chapter? How can you apply it during the next 24 hours?

4. Write a purpose (or good intention) and then write three goals to help you accomplish it.

5. Do you face a task that seems overwhelming? What can you do to overcome paralyzing procrastination?

6. Do your goals aim you toward eternal reward, or just toward earthly achievement?

Chapter 14: Crowns of God's Pleasure

1. How has God shown His faithfulness in your life? Do you make it a point to constantly remind yourself of His faithfulness or do you tend to forget it? What difference do you think it would make in your life if you were constantly reminded of the good things He has done for you? What steps could you take to remind yourself on a regular basis?

2. Write down ten things for which you are genuinely grateful to God.

3. Does the thought of Christ's appearing fill you with joy or fear? If your answer is "fear," what would have to change in your life before you would "love His appearing" and anticipate it with joy?

4. Have you ever "shepherded" anyone? After reading God's job description for shepherds, what (if anything) would you do differently?

5. What lessons can we learn from farming that can help us become more effective witnesses for Christ?

Chapter 15: Olympic Motivation

1. Is there any "luggage" you are hanging onto that weighs you down as you run the race? Ask the Holy Spirit to search your heart and reveal anything that is slowing you down.

2. Figure out how much time you normally spend each day on preparing yourself physically (dressing, grooming, exercising, eating meals). How much time do you spend preparing yourself spiritually? How could you realistically adjust your schedule to improve your spiritual preparation? What training goals can you set to help you win the race?

3. What is the single most important thing you learned from reading this book?

4. Do you know a person or group of people who would benefit from learning about the Judgment Seat? If so, start sharing this truth as God prepares your heart and gives you opportunity.

NOTES

Chapter 2: Take Heed How You Build

1. We do not mean to imply that our sin is irrelevant at the Judgment Seat of Christ. Even though God forgives us, our sin still affects His evaluation of our lives because sin prevents us from doing the very things He rewards. How, for example, can we serve others, perform acts of kindness or witness effectively if we are absorbed in sin and selfishness? First Corinthians 3:9 says, "You are God's field." Sin keeps us from being a *profitable* field. Anything that diminishes the field's fruitfulness also diminishes our reward, whether we rebel willfully or simply let the ground become fallow by neglect. "If any one purifies himself from what is ignoble, then he will be a vessel for noble use, consecrated and useful to the master of the house, ready for any good work" (2 Timothy 2:21).

2. Derek Prince, *The Foundation Series, Book 7: Eternal Judgment* (Derek Prince Ministries International, 1966), p. 33.

3. Stacy and Paula Rinehart, *Living in Light of Eternity* (NavPress, 1986), p. 15.

4. Elisabeth Elliot, *A Chance to Die: The Life and Legacy of Amy Carmichael* (Old Tappan, N.J.: Fleming H. Revell, 1987), p. 31.

5. James Hudson Taylor, *A Retrospect by Hudson Taylor* (Chicago: Moody, 1950), p. 19.

Chapter 3: How Do We Bear Much Fruit?

1. F. F. Bosworth, *Christ the Healer* (Old Tappan, N.J.: Fleming H. Revell, 1973), from the preface.

2. J. I. Packer, *Knowing God* (Downers Grove, Ill.: Inter-Varsity, 1973), pp. 18–19.

3. Hannah Whitall Smith, *The Unselfishness of God* (Princeton, N.J.: Littlebrook, 1987), pp. 136–139.

Chapter 4: Lay Up Treasures in Heaven

1. I had always thought there will be no crying in heaven. I was almost right. Here is what the Bible actually says: "[God] will wipe away every tear from their eyes, and death shall be no more, neither shall there be mourning nor crying nor pain any more, for the former things have passed away" (Revelation 21:4). There will be crying in heaven, but only until God wipes the tears from our eyes.

2. Mark R. Littleton, *Life from the Inside Up* (Denver: Accent, 1991), p. 105.

Chapter 5: The Ultimate Test

1. John Haggai, *Lead On!* (Waco, Tex.: Word, 1986), pp. 54–55.

Chapter 6: Ultimate Success

1. J. C. Ryle, *Practical Religion,* quoted in Packer, *Knowing God,* pp. 156–157.

Chapter 8: The Fear of Man

1. Packer, *Knowing God*, p. 76.

2. Thomas à Kempis, *The Imitation of Christ* (New York: Walker, 1987).

3. Text taken from John Bunyan's *Pilgrim's Progress* and Jim Pappas' adaptation for presentation on cassette (Orion's Gate, P.O. Box 430, Dobbins, CA 95935).

Chapter 9: Developing a Servant's Heart

1. C. S. Lewis, *Mere Christianity* (New York: Macmillan, 1952), p. 114.

2. Hannah Whitall Smith, *The Christian's Secret of a Happy Life* (Old Tappan, N.J.: Fleming H. Revell, 1942), p. 35.

3. Anthony Campolo, *The Kingdom of God Is a Party* (Irving, Tex.: Word, 1990), pp. 3-8.

4. Jesus said that the two greatest commandments are to "love the Lord your God" with all your heart, soul, mind and strength, and to "love your neighbor as yourself" (Mark 12:30–31). Some Christian speakers and writers have said that a third commandment is implied—namely, to love yourself. We cannot love others, they say, until we love ourselves.

Although this interpretation is plausible when examining the text in isolation, it ignores what can be gained from a similar passage in Ephesians 5: "Husbands, love your wives. . . . Husbands should love their wives as their own bodies. . . . For no man ever hates his own flesh, but nourishes and cherishes it. . ." (Ephesians 5:25, 28–29).

Obviously husbands are not being told to love their own bodies first and then to love their wives. Men are being told to show the same thoughtful concern for their wives as they already do for themselves. They are to look out for their wives in the same way that they look out for their own bodies, nourishing and cherishing them.

Let's face it, we are good to ourselves! All of us, including those with low self-esteem, do nice things for ourselves every day. God is not commanding us to love ourselves. We love ourselves already. God is commanding us to lift our focus and treat others with the same thoughtful concern.

5. Edith Schaeffer, *The Hidden Art of Homemaking* (Wheaton, Ill.: Tyndale, 1971), pp. 129–130.

6. Mother Teresa, *Words to Love By* (New York: Walker, 1984), p. 77.

7. Lawrence J. Crabb Jr. and Dan B. Allender, *Encouragement* (Grand Rapids: Zondervan, 1984), pp. 96–97.

8. Hebrews 1:9 says that God anointed Christ with the "oil of joy" because His Son "loved righteousness and hated wickedness" (NIV). Did Christ's joy come from loving others? What does it mean that Christ "loved righteousness"? What is the essence of God's righteous law? Romans 13:9 says that the commandments "are summed up in this sentence, 'You shall love your neighbor as yourself.'" The root of wickedness, on the other hand, is selfishness.

9. Quoted in *The Business Review,* a newsletter published by Kwik Kopy Printing, date unknown.

10. Samuel M. Shoemaker, *By the Power of God* (New York: Harper & Brothers, 1954), p. 67, quoted by James D. Hamilton in *Faces of God* (Kansas City: Beacon Hill, 1984), p. 76.

Chapter 10: Stay Out of His Chair!

1. Pamela Rosewell Moore has authored several books, including *Safer than a Known Way*. She now directs the intercessory prayer ministry at Dallas Baptist University. This text came from one of Pam's talks.

2. Martha Thatcher, *The Freedom of Obedience* (Colorado Springs: NavPress, 1986), p. 65.

Chapter 11: The Fear of the Lord Is a Fountain of Life

1. R. C. Sproul, *The Holiness of God* (Wheaton, Ill.: Tyndale, 1985), pp. 19–20.

2. Joy Dawson, *Intimate Friendship with God* (Grand Rapids: Chosen), p. 24.

3. Text taken from Ethel Barrett's cassette adaptation of *The Holy War* by John Bunyan (Glendale, Calif.: G/L Productions, 1973).

Chapter 12: Pleasing God in Your Work

1. Source unknown.

2. John White, *The Fight* (Downers Grove, Ill.: InterVarsity, 1976), pp. 205–206.

Chapter 13: Seizing the Time

1. Rinehart, *Living,* p. 90.

2. R. Alec Mackenzie, *The Time Trap* (New York: McGraw-Hill, 1971), p. 39.

3. Lewis Timberlake, *Born to Win: You Can Turn Your Dreams into Reality* (Wheaton, Ill.: Tyndale, 1986), p. 138.

4. Alec Mackenzie, *The Time Trap,* 3d ed. (New York: AMACOM, 1997), pp. 41–42.

5. Ted W. Engstrom and R. Alec Mackenzie, *Managing Your Time* (Grand Rapids: Zondervan, 1967), p. 31.

6. Elisabeth Elliot, *Discipline: The Glad Surrender* (Old Tappan, N.J.: Fleming H. Revell, 1982), p. 104.

Chapter 15: Olympic Motivation

1. Jerry White, *The Power of Commitment* (Colorado Springs: NavPress, 1985), p. 18.

Appendix B: The Vision of William Booth

1. William Booth's story was published in tract form many years ago by Life Messengers (Box 1967, Seattle, WA 98111, n.d.). Public domain.

THIS WAS YOUR LIFE!

Video Series and Audio Series Information

Videotaped professionally before a live audience, the video series is broadcast quality, ideal for deepening your understanding and for impacting your church, Sunday school class, home group, youth group, or family members with the life-changing truths of the Judgment Seat of Christ.

The series, taught by both authors, consists of twelve forty-minute teaching sessions along with a Q&A session. Rick Howard has taught on the Judgment Seat of Christ in over eighty countries around the world. Jamie Lash has received three awards on the university level for excellence in teaching.

Each teaching session is followed by questions for group discussion and personal reflection.

For product information, please call 1-800-791-1965 or visit www.LifeGivingWords.com

Rick Howard has pastored Peninsula Christian Center (Redwood City, Calif.) for 27 years. He has written a number of books, two of which are published in over thirty languages.

Jamie Lash is director of student development and professor of economics at a Christian university. He is a popular retreat and conference speaker.

To reach the authors, please contact:

Rick Howard
Peninsula Christian Center
1305 Middlefield Road
Redwood City, CA 94063
1-800-726-3127
fax: 650-368-0790
e-mail: RHoward@pcconline.org
www.pcconline.org/naioth.htm

Jamie Lash
3000 Mountain Creek Parkway
Dallas, TX 75211
214-333-5430
or 1-800-791-1965
fax: 214-333-5430
e-mail: jamie@dbu.edu
www.LifeGivingWords.com